IN GOOD COMPANY
The People of Oxford-On-Rideau

We hope you enjoy this "visit" with the good people of Oxford-On-Rideau.

Elizabeth Irving

Betty Cooper

December 1991

Published by

GENERAL STORE
PUBLISHING HOUSE INC.

1 Main Street, Burnstown, Ontario, Canada K0J 1G0
Telephone (613) 432-7697 or (613) 432-9385

ISBN 0-919431-47-X
Printed and bound in Canada.

Designed by Leanne Enright and Marlene McRoberts

Copyright © 1991
The General Store Publishing House Inc.
Burnstown, Ontario, Canada

Canadian Cataloguing in Publication Data

Irving, Elizabeth
  in good company: the people of oxford-on-rideau

ISBN 0-919431-47-X

  1. Oxford-on-Rideau (Ont.) — Biography. 2. Oxford-on-Rideau (Ont.) — History.
I. Cooper, Betty II. Title.

FC3095.O98Z48 1991 920.0713'73 C91-090478-2 F1059.O982U7 1991

First Printing November 1991

To the good people of Oxford-on-Rideau who have made the township what it is and who are going to preserve its character for the future, we dedicate this book.

ACKNOWLEDGEMENTS

To those who had enough faith in this project to allow us to get it started, we thank you and are grateful for your community spirit.

Specific thanks should be given to the Oxford-on-Rideau Council and to the individuals and groups who kicked in money to get things rolling. Also to Kirk Fachnie who did all the photo processing.

PREFACE

This book has been written to celebrate the tradition of community spirit that is still thriving today in Oxford-on-Rideau Township after 200 years. It salutes contemporary people who contribute their time and talents to help make the township a better place for everyone to live. It's about those who work hard, who lend a hand without asking "What's in it for me?", who set examples young people can follow, who preserve the local heritage, who treat others with respect and good humour when they have nothing else to give. Their values are the same ones that guided and sustained the early settlers in their struggle to tame the land and build a lasting community.

INTRODUCTION

I'd better make two things clear at the start.

First, this is not a history book, although it was partly inspired by history and even contains a good bit of it. *All Around the Township* by Jean Newans, produced in 1984, is the best reference for anyone wanting to know about the past of Oxford-on-Rideau.

Second, the people in the book are just a sample of the men, women, boys and girls, newcomers and old families alike, from all parts of the township, who have helped make Oxford-on-Rideau a great place to live.

The idea for this book first came to me early in 1991, the year of the 200th anniversary of the township's original survey. As publicity person for the new Oxford-on-Rideau Historical Society, I was researching background material for advertising for the first two bicentennial events of the year, a levee in January and a display about life in the first fifty years of the township in February.

I found out that after being surveyed in 1791, Oxford-on-Rideau - ten miles to a side, 30 lots wide and ten concessions deep with the Rideau River as its northern boundary - was slow to be settled because a good deal of the land was originally granted to people who had no intention of pioneering in a rough, undeveloped township. This situation made life harder for legitimate settlers, mostly immigrants from the British Isles, who managed to secure some township land. Although road and land development were the responsibility of individual landowners, absentee owners were not required to contribute to these at all. However, in 1826, a law forced owners to develop their land or give it up. That, along with the opening of the Rideau Canal in 1832, marked the beginning of a population boom for Oxford-on-Rideau. The township flourished and grew as settlers flocked in. Roads, railroads, schools, churches, cheese factories, mills and stores were built to meet the demands and needs of the farming-based community.

If you look beyond these dry facts, you can see something really fascinating: a portrait of the people who came to the raw new land and made a life for themselves.

Virtually all these pioneers came from places with less severe weather and better soil than Eastern Ontario. No matter what drove them to leave their homelands - political or social oppression, or simply a pioneering spirit - they must have been appalled at the harsh, primitive conditions and above all, the isolation. Yet, for various reasons, they stayed and stuck it out, working hard to make life better. Their existence in those very early years must have been constantly lived on a knife-edge of survival. Faith and hope would have been almost tangible.

Once the land opened up, communities quickly formed and the quality of life improved for everyone. Roads soon connected the pockets of settlement that sprang up. Waterways provided power for mills, and so Burritts Rapids, Oxford Mills and Bishops Mills grew by leaps and bounds. Life was hard by today's standards, though not a patch on what the very early people must have suffered. Existence became less iffy and more pleasurable because people could share the work. Community work bees followed by suppers, games and dances became typical forms of entertainment, a combination of work and play for young and old.

People needed other people for survival, and community activities filled the bill. Churches were established and became centres of social as well as religious life. Each succeeding generation built solidly on the knowledge of the one before it; life skills were passed on, and oral history brought awareness of heritage and pride in it. Families stuck together, caring for the elderly and bringing up the young. Neighbours shared what they had with one another. People were responsible and accountable; they were keepers of their fellow man.

The pioneers not only sounded interesting to me - they sounded familiar. Working hard, making do with what you have, co-operating for the good of everyone, helping neighbours, being an active member of church and community, helping and encouraging young people to develop talents and interests, learning and passing on the lessons heritage offers, doing unto others: it was all around me! The same values that kept the pioneers on track are still flourishing in the township today.

Much of the entertainment available today - on television, in films, in reading matter and even in music - glorifies selfishness, greed, ruthlessness, violence and abuse of every description. So, I thought, why not write a book to highlight the good, decent, hard-working, kind, honest people who have helped make the township a better place for everyone? Good people deserve to be honoured and recognized. And the bicentennial provided the perfect framework. Betty Cooper was enthusiastic when I approached her to do the photography for a book about the good people of the township. And so we set to work.

To make our choice of subjects as objective and representative as possible, we consulted with people in community associations, agriculture, education, sports, arts, recreation, schools, churches, entertainment and service clubs. We also talked to people who didn't belong to any of these groups. We called neighbours, friends, friends of friends, acquaintances and even complete strangers for leads. We put a notice in two local papers in March asking for suggestions. From all these sources, we amassed a list of names of individuals and groups for possible inclusion in the book.

Drawing the line was difficult but necessary. We were working within a tight time frame because we wanted the book to be out before the end of the bicentennial year, and so the number of groups and individuals we could cover was limited. At the same time, we also wanted the people we did include to reflect the range and depth of good people in the township.

The two main things we looked for, aside from their having made a contribution of some sort to the community, were that the people in the book be alive and be residents of the township this year. However, we bent the second rule on a few occasions to include former residents, now in nursing and retirement homes in Kemptville and Merrickville, whose personal and family histories are part of the township's heritage.

Meeting the people to interview and photograph them was an enlightening and uplifting experience for both me and Betty. It quickly became apparent to us all that the "ordinary" people we had so blithely referred to in the promotional flyer for the book were anything but ordinary. We were particularly impressed by some of the older people: the wonderful stories they told of days gone by could fill many books. And at times it seemed that everybody was related to nearly everybody else on their mother's side.

The many first-hand accounts we heard of life in the township as far back as the turn of the century. Only reaffirmed that the community spirit we were celebrating was indeed an ongoing tradition in Oxford-on-Rideau.

Corduroy roads were built by early settlers so that horses and wagons could travel through muddy areas. Most of these log structures were taken up or covered when gravel and pavement were put down, but a grass-covered section of corduroy can still be seen behind Harold Bolton's house, where the old road used to run.

For a long time, the best and quickest travelling in the township was done in winter with a horse and cutter. Melvin Weedmark remembers how, near sundown, you could see sleigh tracks shining all the way up the Hoey Road from Actons Corners past Kelly's Corners, more than three miles to the west.

People visited one another a lot in the past, going surprising distances considering the state of the roads. Melvin Weedmark's grandfather used to come to Actons Corners twice a week, year-round, from his farm on County Road 18 near Jig Street. Sometimes the seven-mile trip would take two hours.

Bishops Mills seems to have suffered more than other township communities from temporary isolation caused by impassable roads. According to Lorne Lackie, who retired in 1985 after driving the township grader for nearly 40 years, most of County Road 18 between Oxford Mills and Bishops Mills was not even paved until the late 1970s. Margaret Porter described how several buildings there, including the school, were destroyed by fire in April, 1942, because the fire department could not reach Bishops. Jean Newans, in her days as an itinerant music teacher, could often not negotiate the muddy roads to some of the township's one-room schools, including the one at Bishops. For years Irvine Hough, now 90, had to use a boat to get up his laneway for two or three weeks every spring when the creek flooded.

People almost always made an effort to get together, whether it was for church, for recreational purposes, or for the community work bees which were a pleasant and necessary fact of life until around World War II. Township farmers Ab Storey, Charles Harris, Jay Flannigan and Garnet Tompkins all talked about neighbours joining together to do threshing, sawing and other jobs. Now each farmer does his own work.

Another tradition gone by the wayside is Saturday evening in town which, for farming families, was as much a social occasion as a shopping trip. Stores in Kemptville, Bishops Mills, Burritts Rapids and Oxford Mills would do a brisk business that night. Harold Bolton and his family gravitated to Kidd's store in Burritt's Rapids, and Clifford and Ethel Hutchins headed off to Nottell's store in Bishops. Clifford Hough used to go into Kemptville, the largest centre, and shop at Barnes', Anderson's and Parkinson's. When he was a kid, Ab Storey liked going to the ice cream booth at the Supertest station at the corner of Clothier and Prescott Streets in Kemptville. Sometimes a travelling salesman would peddle his wares there, using a trained black bear to attract customers. In young Theodore Beach's opinion, the best deal around was a half a brick of ice cream at Anderson's in Kemptville for ten cents.

Rita Flannigan remembers the fun they used to have at the Sunday evening euchre parties held turn-about at people's houses. Euchre is still popular, and the Oxford Mills Fellowship Group, started by Sanford Byrd, is considered the best euchre in the area.

The concept of community sports is almost as old as the community itself. Jay Flannigan, like his father before him, used to play ball with his Irishtown neighbours on Sunday afternoons. In the 1930s, as a teenager, Melvin Weedmark played on a mixed Actons Corners ball team which regularly challenged other neighbourhoods about the township. Their ball diamond was usually a pasture, with posts and chicken wire as a temporary backstop.

Community skating rinks, too, are nothing new. Charles Harris was involved in setting up a rink in Oxford Mills in the 1920s, and it continued well into the 1930s. The resourceful organizers ran a power generator with a gas engine to supply lights, and they paid for the gas to run the lights by selling family memberships to the rink.

Lifestyles are very different today from the period represented by these memories. People are more mobile and independent, and they need to rely less on neighbours than in the past. Yet a strong thread of community spirit still binds the population together today. This spirit can be seen in new arrivals and old guard, in children and seniors and those in between, in individuals and families and groups large and small - in all those who contribute what they can to help make life better for everyone.

This book is a tribute to Oxford-on-Rideau Township's most valuable resource, its people.

Elizabeth Irving
November, 1991

IN GOOD COMPANY

The People of Oxford-on-Rideau

NORM AND MILDRED ADAMS
working hard to help community and friends

Music is what first brought Norm and Mildred Adams together. "It's been one thing we've always had in our home and we've taught our two sons," says Norm. Back in the late '30s and early '40s, Norm, a self-taught young musician from Barnard Road in the Todd's School area, played violin and banjo with a group from Oxford Mills. They often came to play for parties in the hall in Bishops Mills. He met Mildred Nottell there when she filled in on the piano with his group a few times. Today, Norm plays violin and banjo with a broader-based country-music group that includes Lorne Beach on the accordion. As often as they can, they play free for the many retirement homes in the area. "The nurses in the manors and nursing homes tell us that the residents really enjoy our music!" says Norm.

Most of Mildred's life has revolved around the general store in Bishops Mills. Her father, W.A. Nottell, ran it until his death in 1945. From 1947 until they sold it in 1975, she and Norm ran it as Adams General Store. Nottell's store carried just about anything a customer might need back then. Rolled oats, flour, soap chips, tea, soda biscuits, harness, hardware and dry goods were all available. The road to Oxford Mills was not paved until the late 1970s, and people at Bishops depended on the local store for most of their needs. Norm and Mildred kept the variety in the store and even added more in paint, wallpaper and floor coverings. "The store seemed to be the hub of the community," says Norm. "Many of our customers were more than customers. They were neighbours and friends."

Mildred was the postmistress for twenty-five years until the Bishops Mills post office was closed in 1970 and residents were put on a rural route out of Oxford Station. The post office was originally installed in Bishops Mills back when stage-coaches used to come up from Prescott, explains Mildred. For many years, when her dad ran the store, the location of the post office would move after an election if the party in power changed. After they sold the store, Norm ran for township council. He spent six years as a councillor and another six as deputy reeve. Norm remembers how well council members and staff worked together in those years. "And it was through co-operation between township and county council that we were able to have the sidewalks rebuilt and new gutters and aprons added along the roads in Bishops in time for the centennial celebration there in 1985," he says.

Both Mildred and Norm have helped out with functions in connection with St. Andrew's United Church, and Mildred has belonged for years to the United Church Women. She meets often with two other village residents, Joan Robinson and Noreen Brown, to make quilts. When the Bishops Mills Women's Institute was revived in 1985, Mildred was a charter member and has served as treasurer and assistant district director.

On his living-room wall Norm keeps three awards: one from the township in recognition of his service to Oxford-on-Rideau from 1977 to 1988, a Certificate of Merit from the Government of Canada in 1988 for his contribution to his community, and an appreciation from Leeds and Grenville in 1988 for his six years of service on county council.

CLARENCE ARCAND
helping to keep the township safe for everyone

Clarence Arcand has helped make Oxford-on-Rideau a safer place to live through his long involvement in conservation and animal control. An avid hunter and fisherman, Clarence is also interested in keeping local animal populations healthy so that they do not become a nuisance or danger to residents.

Since 1979, Clarence has been the township's by-law enforcement officer, a job he shares with one of his seven children, Gary. Most of his work involves acting on residents' complaints about stray animals, usually dogs. "It's a thankless job," he chuckles.

For years, Clarence has kept township municipal drains open by trapping beaver and dynamiting their dams. At the moment, he explains, beaver are numerous because the low price for their fur gives little incentive to trappers. "I've been blowing dams for quite a while," says Clarence, who has noticed an increase in beaver numbers lately.

When he retired in 1975 after fifteen years as custodian at Holy Cross School, Clarence had more time to devote to hunting and fishing. However, his interest goes beyond mere participation in these sports; he also spends a lot of time improving conditions for other sportsmen, for local residents and for the animals themselves.

Through the Grenville-Carleton Sportsman and Conservation Club, where he spent five years as president, Clarence operated a fish hatchery for several years at his home on the Kemptville Creek. In conjunction with the Ministry of Natural Resources, he and the club raised the tiny fry to the fingerling stage and released them in the Rideau River. The club's current project is enhancing the pickerel beds in the Rideau River at Burritts Rapids by washing the silt off the rocks with fire hoses so that the pickerel eggs can then lodge safely between the rocks, to hatch away from predators.

Clarence is now president of the Anglers and Hunters Zone 4. This group's Eastern Ontario chapter is dedicated to protecting wetlands and fighting water pollution. The association also works closely with the Ministry of Natural Resources in looking after the environment. "We try everything," he says.

Clarence has also been instrumental in greatly improving relations between residents and deer hunters in Oxford-on-Rideau township over the last few years. He was one of the founders of the Hunters' Council which encourages hunters to obey the laws and respect the wishes and private property of landowners. Before the council was set up, hunters had a poor image with non-hunting residents. "It only takes one bad hunter to ruin it for everyone," explains Clarence. Since the hunters have been policing themselves through the Hunters' Council, the number of complaints during deer-hunting season has dropped dramatically.

THEODORE BEACH
an all-round gentleman

Ask anybody who has been around the township for a while to name the most highly respected man in Oxford-on-Rideau. Chances are they'll point to Theodore Beach and cite as their reasons his honesty and fairness as a businessman and politician and his kindness and generosity as a friend and neighbour.

Born on the Beach Road farm his grandfather bought in 1875 (where his younger brother, Lorne, lives now), Protestant Theodore went to school and played softball at predominantly Catholic Irishtown. He realized at a very young age that religious affiliations "make no difference. People are people."

His father, Theodore Senior, had dealt in dairy cows all his life, but Theodore found himself more interested in beef cattle. His future career as a drover was established firmly in 1932 when he bought his first cow for $2.50 and sold it for $3.00. "I had in my mind at ten years old that that was what I was going to do: buy cattle and ship them." In all his years as a drover, he never lost interest in the work. One reason, he says, was his ability and intense interest in arithmetic.

Theodore carefully saved all his money, and by 1939, when he was sixteen, he had amassed $500, enough to buy a scale house at Bedell. He had to use a horse and cutter in the winters for several years because the roads were so bad. "I'd leave in the morning," he recalls, "and be out all day in the cutter buying stuff."

After he married Lilah Barkley of South Mountain in 1942, they moved into a stone house down the road from the family farm. "This is as far as I've ever got," Theodore chuckles. Like most residents back then, the Beaches led a self-sufficient life out of necessity. Lilah did a good share of the farm work because Theodore spent long days away on the job. For the first three years of their marriage, the house had no electrical service, but that was no hardship at the time. Life was simple and direct: they raised and butchered their own meat, grew their own vegetables, and canned both in sealers to last the winter.

Theodore's work put him in contact with people all over Oxford-on-Rideau and further afield as well. "I can guarantee you I knew every person in the township at one time," he says. People welcomed him into their homes to do business for more than his good company: they knew he was trustworthy and would keep to himself any details of their private family matters that might come to his attention. His habit of respecting the privacy of others is still strong today.

From 1968 through 1988, Theodore spent twenty-one consecutive years on the Oxford-on-Rideau township council, the first fifteen as a councillor, and the last six as reeve. When he first sat on council, he was instrumental in getting a second township grader to make the roads much more accessible in winter. "That second grader, to me, was the most wonderful thing!"

On Theodore's family-room wall hang two awards. One, a Certificate of Merit from the government of Canada, dated February 26, 1988, is inscribed "In grateful recognition of your contribution to your community." The other is a Certificate of Merit from Oxford-on-Rideau council, awarded in March 1989 "in recognition of the many hours spent in serving the residents of Oxford-on-Rideau."

LUELLA BECKETT
a love of mankind and simple pleasures

At ninety-three, Mrs. Luella Beckett enjoys the quiet, comfortable life she leads in her retirement apartment at Bayfield Manor. Certainly the pace is much different from when she and her husband Cecil started building up Becketts Landing into the area's major summer resort nearly seventy years ago.

Mrs. Beckett, the daughter of William Harnett, was born June 15, 1898, on the north side of the Rideau River in Marlborough Township. One of her earliest memories is of the Harnetts' house being moved away from the river, with a winch and rollers, when she was about four. The family continued to live in the house during the move which took several days.

In 1916, at age eighteen, she married Cecil Beckett from Oxford-on-Rideau Township on the south side of the river. The first Beckett, Nathaniel, came to Canada in 1819. The Beckett family farm, located on what is now South River Road, was started by Cecil's grandfather, James Beckett. Cecil took over the farm while his father, Lieutenant Colonel David Beckett, was in the Home Guard after World War I. "I was the third Mrs. Beckett that lived in that house," she recalls. After nine years on the farm, she and Cecil bought their own land near the river at Becketts Landing, about a mile from the farm.

In those days, there was a swing bridge across the Rideau River, west of where the present bridge is now. Not far from the old bridge, in a prime location on the main highway leading north from Kemptville to Ottawa, Cecil and Luella built their new home. It included a store, a snack-bar and a lunch-room, and there were boat docks and gas pumps there as well.

While their three children, Marjorie, Lorena and Earl, were growing up, Mrs. Beckett catered to the tourist trade. In 1937, the present bridge was built, and the highway was relocated a quarter mile further east to join up with it. When the old bridge was dismantled, Becketts Landing continued to attract swimmers and fishermen on Sundays even though it was no longer on the beaten path.

Cecil drew the mail between Kemptville and Burritts Rapids for eighteen years when they lived at Becketts Landing and later, after they moved to Kemptville, for another eighteen years. Cecil passed away the winter after his eightieth birthday.

The resort at Becketts Landing changed hands several times after the Becketts sold it in 1950. Eventually, the various commercial enterprises were closed down one by one, and the area became residential. The Becketts' house is still there.

(L - R): Dwight, James, Erma, Melissa, Andrew, Rosemary holding Zachary, Charles holding Sarah

THE BENNETT FAMILY
looking to the future in farming

"If you like what you do," says Dwight Bennett, "you try to do it well." In an economic climate when many farmers are reducing their operations or getting out of farming altogether, the Bennetts of South River Road are meeting the crunch head on with a tough optimism. Their faith in farming can be seen in the new barn they built in 1990.

"We wouldn't be expanding if our sons were not involved," says Dwight Bennett. Both Charles and James are full partners with him in the dairy operation. After the new free-stall barn with milking parlor was completed, they added to their registered Rideauside Holstein herd; they now milk 120 cows and have the capacity to go up to two hundred. Most of the 450 acres they cultivate belong to the family.

"When we came here thirty-six years ago, there were fifteen (dairy farms) on this road between (Highway) 16 and Merrickville, and now there's two," Dwight observes. He and Erma bought the farm and moved there as newly-weds. Dwight continued to work days at RCA Victor in Prescott for eight years, and during that time they started to build up the farm and began their family of five children. In 1963, Dwight and Erma went into full-time milk production, adding a bulk tank so that Borden would give them twenty-five cents more a hundredweight for their milk.

Charles, their older son, returned from the Ontario Agricultural College in Guelph with a diploma in 1976. From that point until last year's expansion, the Bennetts kept a closed herd, breeding their own new cows rather than buying them at the sale barn. James, too, has his diploma from Kemptville College.

The Bennett farm is a family-run operation with one full-time hired man and occasional relief milkers on weekends. At peak work times, spring and fall, they often work past dark to get everything done. Erma keeps the farm books and Rosemary, Charles' wife, registers the calves.

Dwight has been an active member of a number of agricultural associations including the Soil and Crop Improvement Association, the Ontario Dairy Herd Improvement Corporation, the Grenville Milk Committee, the Grenville Holstein Club and the Ontario Milk Marketing Board. He is presently on the Farm Products Marketing Commission. "I've had my fling at these and now Charles is involved with several clubs," says Dwight.

For six years, Dwight served Oxford-on-Rideau as a public school-board trustee. Both he and Erma have been active members of the United Church, in Burritts Rapids until it closed, and, more recently, in Oxford Mills; Erma was the last president of the Burritts Rapids United Church Women. In her long association with the Women's Institute, she is a past provincial board director and is currently second vice-president of the eastern area. Rosemary has served as a 4-H leader, was involved in the setting up of the Kemptville Co-operative Nursery School, and is now in her second year as director of the County Federation of Agriculture. She is also an active member of the Agriculture Awareness Committee, whose main focus is Agriculture in the Class-room, a program to teach school children more about farming and food production.

MELVIN AND WILLA BLACK
a leading family at Oxford Station

In 1875, Melvin Black's grandfather, William John, built the stone house on a hundred and fifty stony acres on Black Road where three generations of Blacks would farm for a living for over a century. However, the first generation there was a short one: before the new house was even completely furnished, William John died. Simon, the second youngest of his nine children, came home from Regina to help his mother run the family farm. Simon had four children. Minnie (now Mrs. Lawrence Pelton of Kemptville) taught school for many years; Claire worked with CP Telegraph in Montreal; Melvin went into the cheese business; and Whitney carried on the farm. It was sold when Whitney's son John chose another line of work.

Melvin can remember a time when there were eighty-nine cheese factories within a fifty-mile radius of Oxford Station. Two of those belonged to James A. Sanderson, who started up a wholesale cheese-exporting business at Oxford Station in the late 1920s. Melvin was hired on to work in the office in 1936, and he was employed there until 1967. Prior to the Sandersons' selling the business to the Ontario Milk Marketing Board in 1963, the government had stopped exporting cheese through Oxford Station and most of the local cheese factories had closed down. Melvin continued in the cheese business, commuting to Winchester till his retirement in 1982.

He had just stepped down from the work-force when he was approached to run for township council in Oxford-on-Rideau. He recalls the six years he served as councillor as a time of great co-operation within the council. Two thorny issues — a rock quarry on Hwy 43 and the Van Camp Drain — were successfully resolved near the beginning of his political career. "The first two years I wondered why I had run!" he laughs. He retired from council in 1988 at the age of seventy-four. More recently, he and Willa, his wife of fifty-one years, moved from rural Oxford Station to the south side of Kemptville.

When she married Melvin, Willa Carson, also from the Oxford Station area, had already graduated in nursing from the Grace Hospital in Ottawa. For some years she did private nursing and later worked at Kemptville District Hospital. Willa became a Registered Nurse and retired in 1971.

Both Melvin and Willa have given a lot of their time and energy over the years to make life better for Oxford-on-Rideau residents. During the '60s, Melvin served on the Kemptville District Hospital Board for nine years, two as chairman. "It was an honour to be on it," he says. Both he and Willa used to canvass regularly for the heart and cancer funds in Oxford Station, and they are still active in the United Church in Heckston where Willa belongs to the United Church Women and the choir. Melvin volunteers his services driving cancer patients to clinics in Ottawa and delivering food to house-bound seniors through Meals on Wheels. Willa was Kemptville Hospital's very first co-ordinator of volunteers, regularly donating her own efforts with the rest. She has a long-standing record of volunteer service at Bayfield Manor, and is presently treasurer of the Bayfield Auxiliary. In 1989, Willa received an award from the township of Oxford-on-Rideau in recognition of her community work.

HAROLD BOLTON
bringing the past to life through oral history

Harold Bolton has a wealth of knowledge about the history of his home turf and, to go with it, a trick of making the past come alive when he talks.

Harold has lived his entire eighty years in the house where he was born on what is now known as Bolton Road. The log house was built by his grandfather Samuel Bolton. Samuel's father, Richard Bolton, came from Ireland in 1834 to settle on Crown land at Dales Creek, just west of part of the present Bolton farm. Naomi Horning, Harold's mother, was of United Empire Loyalist stock.

When Harold was a schoolboy at SS No 5, Gibson's School, on the Scotch Line, trains stopped regularly at Burritt Station, where the track crosses Bolton Road, to pick up passengers, milk and anything else to be shipped as far as Montreal. The Scotch Line was the usual route to Merrickville then, before the Hoey Road, now called Hwy 43, was put through in 1950. Around 1889, Harold's father and grandfather used to draw milk from seventeen farms along the Scotch Line between Burritt Station and Merrickville. "The farmers made a good living on those rocks," says Harold.

Burritts Rapids was where the Boltons did most of their shopping. Harold's wife Ruth worked at Kidd's Store there for years. "You could buy anything from a knitting needle to a horse harness," he recalls. At one point, Burritts Rapids had a grist mill, a woollen mill, a cheese factory, two blacksmith shops and three gas pumps — Esso, Shell and Red Indian.

The Boltons were dairy farmers. Harold milked till the '70s and then sold the quota. He often worked off the farm too. From 1945 to 1953, he worked at Grenville Castings in Merrickville for his brother-in-law Roy Pevere, and he drove a snow-plough for the Department of Highways in the 1960s. When he worked on the Rideau Canal as a carpenter from 1968 to 1976, he helped build two swing bridges, including the one at Andrewsville. He has done a good bit of house construction, especially for friends and relatives, and last year, he worked on his own roof.

Harold's grandparents helped out with the building of the Methodist Church at Newmanville in 1877, the same year Harold's father was born. The Bolton family supported the church actively until the building was closed in 1950 and subsequently torn down. The family switched to the United Church in Merrickville.

Harold remembers picking blueberries in the Huckleberry Marsh just west of Bolton Road. The blueberries flourished after a huge fire in the early 1900s devastated a large area. "I remember the men talking about the fire," says Harold. "They had to cut a ditch to the east to stop it." The berries were productive until fairly recently. "They're history now," he says, after a recent foray into the bog turned up a very sad crop of berries.

CORA AND SANFORD BYRD
community-minded citizens by any definition

Cora and Sanford Byrd joke about coming to Oxford-on-Rideau Township in 1939 "with a three-tinted cow and a balky horse." Before that, the young couple had lived in Winchester and Brinston since 1936 when Sanford had married Cora Bartholomew of Inkerman. He had grown up in the Hallville area although his great-grandparents William Burd and Maria Batterby had settled at Aultsville, one of the "lost" villages on the St. Lawrence, when they came over from England in 1842.

Sanford was "mainly a farmer," but he almost always supplemented the farming with other work. In the 1930s, he took a hairdressing course in Ottawa. "I worked at that at night and worked for a farmer in the daytime," he recalls. He charged twenty-five cents for a neck trim, thirty-five cents for a finger wave and $1.25 for a permanent wave under the old clamp dryer. Later, he used to cut wood in Limerick and haul it with a team of horses to Swedlove's in Kemptville where he got three dollars for three cords. "You'd bring it all home in a box of groceries," says Sanford. "We call them the good old times, but I don't think we'd want to trade!"

Until 1966, they farmed on Limerick and O'-Neill Roads. The land was poor, and Sanford drove trucks and school buses while their three sons were growing up. "We ploughed the whole east half of Oxford Township with one truck," he says of the early 1960s when he worked for the township. Cora worked for the Ministry of Natural Resources for thirty-four years, retiring in 1985.

Both Sanford and Cora are long-time members of Oxford Mills United Church. Cora has held many offices with the United Church Women and is just completing a term as president, not her first. In 1971, Sanford and Mr. (Ross) Stevenson instigated the finishing of the basement in the United Church. "We had to lower it and scrape it all out by hand. But it's really paid off. We have everything there but the euchres."

Cora has put her talent for newspaper reporting to work. For many years she has written up the Oxford Mills area news for the Kemptville *Advance*, and she is presently the Public Relations Officer for the Oxford Mills branch of the Women's Institute which she joined in 1965.

One of Sanford's greatest joys in life is collecting just about anything, as his home and barn attest. Plates, pictures, tools, books, lanterns and even exotic birds have all had their place in his life. He has been very generous with his belongings, lending "anything they want" to the Kemptville Players to utilize as props and costumes in their productions.

In 1989, Sanford was presented with an award from Oxford-on-Rideau township for helping to establish the Oxford Mills Fellowship Group in 1968, for transporting seniors from Oxford Mills to recreational programs in Kemptville, and for being a founding member of the Oxford-on-Rideau Community Association. "I'm the type of guy who can't say no," he admits. "I'll help anyone."

PETER AND MARGARET CARSON
sharing the wonder of God's creatures

Peter and Margaret Carson are crazy about birds and animals. But this only partially explains why they keep hundreds of creatures, many rare and exotic and most beloved pets, on their hundred-acre retirement farm east of Oxford Mills.

To anyone meeting the Carsons, it quickly becomes apparent that the people and adventures they encounter through their hobby are just as dear to them as the birds and animals themselves.

Just having a tour of the sanctuary is a pleasure, but often, when the Carsons aren't too busy, visitors can sample Margaret's wonderful pie and listen to some of Peter's endlessly entertaining stories. A favourite is about the time the ostrich ran away from home. In 1985, their male South American ostrich, possibly rebelling at being named Lady Di, managed to escape. He was apparently sighted as far away as Almonte and Perth before returning home of his own accord eleven days later. Peter also likes to tell about the time their cross Cape Baron goose chased Wayne Rostad down the lane when he was filming a segment for Country Report.

The Carsons lived in Ottawa and used the farm as a weekend retreat until 1979 when they moved there permanently. Since then, they have been seriously collecting their wide variety of birds and animals. They even installed a mile-long creek, complete with islands, for their water fowl. "I did it with a high hoe," explains Peter. They have been working in co-operation with Ducks Unlimited for several years. In 1990, that organization installed a dam on the Carsons' property to enhance the habitat for water fowl.

Peter and Margaret were instrumental in starting the Oxford-on-Rideau Bird Club in 1986 when it became apparent that there were a lot of bird fanciers in the area but no local organization. Aside from promoting birds and bringing together people of similar interests, the club imports birds for auctions.

"I tell everyone I make money out of the birds, but that's a lie," confides Peter. But having their birds and animals and being able to share them with others far outweighs the expense and time the Carsons invest in their stock. They often supply birds in cages to display at bird shows and events such as the fiftieth anniversary of the Ministry of Natural Resources held at Limerick Forest in 1990. On that occasion, they brought along Canada geese, mallard and other water fowl.

Schools, churches and organizations such as Brownies and Guides have all been treated to tours and refreshments at the farm. In 1989, twelve hundred children from Barrhaven Public School, delivered in bus loads over a period of time, all visited the farm. "Fine children," recalls Peter. "They were really good."

Peter and Margaret also enjoy displaying some of their birds and animals on floats in parades. Peter remembers one of their first parades, held in Oxford Mills during the 1967 centennial celebrations. "I was the bride," he laughs. "I had the little donkey drawing us in a buggy."

HELEN CHECKLEY
a life devoted to those in need

Helen Checkley is carrying on a tradition with her activities around Burritts Rapids.

Before her husband Earle passed away in 1988, the couple acted as a strong community-minded team over the years. Although Earle was more often in the forefront, Helen was behind him one hundred per cent in all his endeavours. "We worked together on practically everything," says Helen. In the 1970s, they were involved with the development of the Burritts Rapids branch of the Oxford-on-Rideau Public Library and helped install metal shelving in both township library branches. Earle was on the township library board for eight years. Both served on the Burritts Rapids Community Hall Corporation board for years, Earle as chairman for a while. They did everything from helping with the twice-monthly bingos to taking their turn as hall janitors. In 1988, Earle was presented with a Volunteer Service Award from the provincial government for his community work. In 1989, he was posthumously awarded a Certificate of Merit from the township of Oxford-on-Rideau.

Helen can actually take double credit for the new kitchen that was put into the hall because it was jointly sponsored by the hall board and the local Women's Institute. Helen held every office possible in her twenty-year membership in the Burritts Rapids Women's Institute before the chapter was disbanded in 1988. She also belonged to the Burritts Rapids United Church Women, a group which carried on in and about the village until 1989, even though the church was closed in 1974.

To help keep the Merrickville District Community Health Centre in good repair, Helen represents Oxford-on-Rideau Township on its board of directors. She took over the job from Earle who had been treasurer of this group for years and had also been instrumental in its survival.

These days, the better part of Helen's time is devoted to improving the quality of life for seniors. She has been involved as a co-ordinator and a volunteer driver with the Smiths Falls Friends for Seniors for three years. "I take people on jaunts rather than just medical appointments," she says, knowing how much the seniors enjoy a break from their routines.

Helen is in her second year as president of the Burritts Rapids New Horizons Club for seniors, which meets every two weeks. "We're quite an active group," she explains, "for the most part younger than some of the other seniors' groups in the area." The New Horizons Club, through its government grant, was responsible for putting a new roof on the Burritts Rapids Community Hall and for installing a new ceiling in the old wing.

Helen recently donated a replica of an old school wall clock to the hall in her late husband's name.

(*=resident of Oxford-on-Rideau)

Back Row (L - R): *Myron Mills, Sid McGrath, *George Argus, *Art Munro, Stanley Ralph, *Sanford Byrd, Arthur Fisher, *Henry De Haan

Middle Row (L - R): Wilhelmina Doef, Betty Gault, Marion Harasimo, *Marg Rupert, Joan Fisher, *Jean Hamlyn, Agatha Ralph

Front Row (L - R): Fran Chambers, *Val Kirkwood, *Martha Sladek, Arlene McKibbon, *Jean Newans, Sandi Tillbury, Eleanor Simonyi, Nancy Holmes, *Jean Sears

Not Shown: *Cheryl Morgan

COMMUNITY CHOIR
sharing a love of music

Oxford-on-Rideau's community choir was born in 1984, the year of Ontario's bicentennial. "I'd always thought about a choir," says Jean Newans, who started the group in early 1984 to provide a musical component for the different events planned for that year.

About thirty-five people came out to the initial practices. The choir's very first public performance was on St. Patrick's Day in 1984. The Ceilidh Band, an Ottawa musical group, gave a performance to a huge audience at Oxford-on-Rideau School, and the choir got into the Gaelic spirit with such pieces as "The Rose of Tralee" and "An Irishman's Idea of Love." They continued to sing at different community events throughout the year, gaining confidence and skill with each performance.

"Jean is the heart and soul of the choir," says Myron Mills, a veteran member of the group. As choir director, Jean runs a tight ship, settling for nothing less than the best efforts of everyone involved, regardless of their singing ability. "If you like to sing, you can fit in," says Jean. Everyone is welcome to join. Some members come from Merrickville and even Smiths Falls, although most are from the township.

Regular choir practices are held Tuesday evenings from October to June at the school in Oxford Mills. Although Jean is an accomplished pianist, she prefers to have an accompanist so that she can give her full attention to the singing. Mimi Churma, the regular organist at St. Anne's Catholic Church in Merrickville, is the present accompanist.

Since 1984, the choir has continued to meet and perform at a variety of functions, both religious and secular. "The type of songs we sing just depends on where we get invited," explains Jean. They go to a number of area churches to present their Christmas and Easter programs, and have performed twice at both the South Gower cemetery service and the muscular-dystrophy telethon in Smiths Falls. They staged two well-attended concerts, with other musical performances, in 1990 and 1991. The choir was also on hand for the official designation of the Oxford-on-Rideau town hall as a heritage building in June 1991.

There is no typical member of the choir; the group represents an interesting cross-section of the community. Men and women of all ages and degrees of ability in music are from diverse backgrounds: teachers, ministers, farmers, plumbers, politicians, homemakers, secretaries and more find a common denominator in music.

(L - R): John Foster (reeve), Jean Hamlyn (deputy reeve), Ken MacDougall,
Mel Johnston, Nancy Curtis

COUNCIL
giving of themselves for the betterment of Oxford-on-Rideau Township

In December 1988, Reeve John Foster, Deputy Reeve Jean Hamlyn, and Councillors Nancy Curtis, Mel Johnston and Ken MacDougall were sworn in for a term that included Oxford-on-Rideau's bicentennial year.

Since the township's first council was elected in 1850, every council has had its own particular issues to deal with, some of them thorny. But one thing all councils have had in common is frustration at having to forgo certain projects and programs because too little money was available. Now, with the education portion of ratepayers' tax bills higher than ever, council is loath to add to that burden. Thus any potential spending receives careful consideration so that as many residents as possible can benefit from money paid out.

Here are some of the things the present council has done to benefit the community during 1989, 1990 and 1991:

Road Superintendant Lee Seabrook and Assistant Road Superintendant Doug Scott have continued with the repair and rehabilitation of township bridges in accordance with the very high standard demanded by council. The most recent to be upgraded was the Dennison Road bridge. Roads are regularly maintained, and the paving program continues when funds allow. Protective safety devices are being installed at all level railway crossings. And to make sure that Totem Ranch Road is accessible once it is dead-ended by the future Hwy 416, council has negotiated with the Ministry of Transportation for an access road connecting it to Oxford Station Road.

In the past, the township has purchased fire protection service from the Kemptville Fire Department without having any share in the management of the service. In 1991, council set up a joint board of management for future services.

The new official plan that council adopted in 1989 sets out broad guide-lines for the development of the township over the next ten to fifteen years. There can be no doubt that Oxford-on-Rideau is on the verge of a population explosion, and council hopes to minimize its impact on existing residents. The plan has been presented to ratepayers at a series of meetings, and their complaints and comments have been taken into account in amendments made to it. Although the plan has circulated through various ministries, it is still lacking approval by the Ministry of Municipal Affairs.

The start of a recycling program, concentrated at the Oxford Mills waste-disposal site, is one of the big additions to the township's two landfills. Council, faced with long-term planning for waste, will be hiring consultants to advise on the most efficient use of the area they have. They will also be purchasing the equipment to cover and compact waste to prolong the lives of the two sites.

Council has participated in the Kemptville-Oxford-South Gower (KOSOG) study on area recreation needs and expects to take part in joint action in the near future. Meanwhile, some money is being made available for groups and programs already established in the township.

JOHN CURTIS
leadership through education

No one is more aware of the latest trends in agriculture and the food industry than John Curtis. As principal of Kemptville College of Agricultural Technology for the last seventeen years, John has been making sure the programs offered by the college meet the needs of the people of Eastern Ontario. "Agriculture is not a growth industry," he says. "I think you've just got to tell these kids the truth."

When John became principal in 1974, the college offered diplomas in two areas: agriculture, and food and fashion. But changing times have brought different training needs which the college must address. "As we improve (farming) efficiency, we need fewer and fewer farm managers," explains John. Our demand for food has not increased along with our ability to produce it. As a result, John has made significant changes in the college diploma programs. Agriculture, once the mainstay of the college, is being cut back, with emphasis given to other areas. "I think our programs will expand and benefit the community," says John.

Thanks to the diversification that John has introduced into the college programs, overall enrollment has not dropped and graduates are highly employable. Students in the food service program now step into jobs as assistant dietitians for health-care facilities such as hospitals and nursing homes. Agricultural welders and farm-equipment mechanics, tick-

eted by the federal government, can work anywhere in Canada. Graduates of the horse program become riding instructors recognized by the Equestrian Association of Canada. Ornamental landscaping is also on the rise, and international training enables people from around the world to share our advanced agricultural techniques. Agriculture now concentrates on dairy because it is "our main industry in the Valley," explains John.

"I was raised on a beef farm in St. Thomas, Ontario," says John. He married Nancy Tuck of Hamilton-Burlington right after he graduated from Guelph with a BSc in Agriculture. He worked as a soils and crops specialist at Ridgetown until 1963 when he received his MSc in corn production from Guelph. He then taught crop science at Ridgetown until 1966 when he was hired by Kemptville Agricultural School. A year later, it became known as Kemptville College of Agricultural Technology, the change in name signalling a change in emphasis from straight teaching to teaching and research. In October 1974, he became principal after Dr. Ford Stinson retired.

John believes that the days are past when a love of the work, the land and the animals is enough to keep a farmer going. Today's farm managers must be sharp business people to make it, and he is making sure that Kemptville College gives them the best possible education to do this.

VICTOR AND LINDA DESROCHES
working together to build community spirit

In the sixteen years that Victor and Linda Desroches have lived in the village of Bishops Mills, they have donated a good deal of time and effort to help boost culture and recreation in Oxford-on-Rideau. Victor grew up in Lafontaine, Ontario, a small village near Georgian Bay. "That's where I learned the importance of getting involved with the community," he says. Linda, an Ottawa native, shares his view that the more people contribute to the community, the richer life will be for everyone in it.

A librarian by profession, Victor first shared his expertise with the community by starting up a small library in Bishops Mills in 1976. At that time, the only library in the township was located at Burritts Rapids, some ten miles away. "We collected all kinds of donations from people around here," he recalls. Burritts Rapids lent them new acquisitions regularly, as well. The library is still open and local residents use it on an honour system. In 1983, Victor joined the Oxford-on-Rideau Library Board, and he has just stepped down after three years as chairman.

A year of great significance in Bishops Mills was 1985, the village's centennial year. The Desroches, like so many others in the village, helped plan and organize a very successful celebration. Interest in holding the event "took off like a brush fire," says Victor, and it proved to have a cohesive effect on the community. One spin-off initiative from the centennial celebration was a community project, with the help of a provincial grant, to repair and refurbish the old Temperance Hall.

Through the Bishops Mills Community Association, Victor, Linda and others have obtained government grants and expanded and upgraded the local park with a new service building, playground equipment, landscaping and other improvements. The association plans community events such as winter-fun days, Hallowe'en and Christmas parties, ball games and potluck suppers.

Linda has been a representative for the Bishops Mills area on the Oxford-on-Rideau Recreation Association for six years. This group has been responsible for township-wide programs for children such as summer fun and gymnastics. She is also a founding member of the Bishops Mills Women's Institute where she has served on the executive as vice-president and public-relations officer. When their two children, Melanie, twelve, and Jason, fifteen, were younger, Linda was a mother helper at Brownies, and both a parent volunteer and a member of the parent school committee at Holy Cross school.

ALBERT AND INA DYKS
sharing life's blessings

Albert and Ina Dyks have been a quiet, steady source of support to the community and to each other since they moved to Oxford-on-Rideau Township in 1964. "The Lord has blessed us and we can give something back," explains Albert. "We share our blessings."

The Dyks family has enjoyed a long association with the Christian Reform Church. Albert is currently an elder, and he has held this position and that of deacon in the past. Ina has served as president and secretary of the Ladies Society, a church Bible study group. Over the years, the home-based business she and Albert have operated together since 1972 pretty well took care of any spare time she had while their three children, Patti, Lisa and Derek, were growing up.

A charter member of the Kemptville Kinsmen Club, Albert was invited to join the Lions Club about seven years ago. He is now second vice-president, a position which will lead to the presidency. Albert's own pet fund-raising project, a contribution to the Lions' ongoing support of the Canadian National Institute for the Blind, is selling ice-cream Yule-logs with the local Kinnettes.

Committee work rather than fund raising has been Albert's specialty in the twelve years he has served on the Kemptville and District Hospital Board. He has been part of just about every committee going and has recently retired from the executive where his last position was past president. He sees frequent leadership changes as healthy. "New people, new ideas — it doesn't get stale that way."

Buenavista on the Rideau, a Merrickville rehabilitation centre for the treatment of drug and alcohol abuse, has also benefitted from Albert's attention. For several years he was chairman of the board which takes care of the building and makes decisions on the operation of the facility. He eventually had to drop this project. "I was just too involved with the hospital and I couldn't devote the time that was needed for both."

For both Albert and Ina, religion is a big part of their lives, but they also believe in having a good time and enjoying life. They are living examples of the successful balancing of laughter and relaxation with duty and hard work.

"You try to help your community and your fellow man as much as you can," says Albert.

TONI EARLE EMSLIE
a love of creatures great and small

Toni Emslie's life has always revolved around her love of animals. In the twenty-four years that she has lived near Oxford Station, she has rescued many orphaned domestic and wild animals and birds, often in co-operation with the Ministry of Natural Resources, caring for them in her kitchen until they were well enough to be released safely back into their habitats. "My survival rate is nearly 100%," she says of the motley collection of creatures she has fostered. Baby squirrels, racoons, groundhogs, rabbits and foxes have all been guests under her brooder lamp, as have more exotic bird species such as a great grey owl, a red-shouldered hawk, an American kestrel and a budgie.

Toni took a course years ago in wildlife management, given in Montreal, and she is a member of the Wildlife Orphan Rescue Fund. This organization, based in Constance Bay, places homeless baby animals and birds in temporary shelters in private homes. Toni also acts as an unofficial rescue centre for abandoned or abused cats and dogs.

Toni knows what it's like to be attached to a pet and devastated when it eventually dies, and she has tried to make this situation easier for other pet owners. At the front of her property, Toni has set aside two acres for Oxford-on-Rideau's first and only public pet cemetery. Presided over by a statue of St. Francis of Assisi, the patron saint of animals, the ground was blessed by the Reverend Don Spencer-Lee. "A lot of people in the community had been asking me if I'd start a pet cemetery," she explains. She set it up in 1985, realizing the need for this service after the sudden death of her beloved champion Arabian stallion. Currently, five horses are buried there, including three from the Moscow circus, victims of rhino- pneumonia while in Canada.

Toni has kept many animals as pets, including horses, pygmy goats and ferrets. When it comes to animal breeding, her goal is to produce healthy, good-natured, trainable family pets. For seven years, she was Eastern Ontario's biggest ferret breeder, and the animals she bred from reliable American stock, became very popular as pets.

"Dogs are my main thing," Toni admits. She has trained and shown many different breeds over the years. In her view, a dog that is not trained is not a happy dog, and its owners will probably be unhappy with it as well. She is actively involved, through public talks and seminars, in raising public awareness of the necessity of having properly trained dogs. Abuse or abandonment of dogs often results when their untrained behavior encroaches on the comfort and convenience of humans. Most problems in dogs' behavior are man-made, she says. Meanwhile, she is working on making the community a better place for dogs and people to coexist.

LARRY AND ANSTACE ESMONDE-WHITE
delighting in sharing the beauty they create

Larry and Anstace Esmonde-White love people and gardening. Since moving to Evergreen Farm on Bedell Road in 1972, the couple has devoted a lot of time to bringing the two loves together by promoting gardening for the enjoyment and good health it can bring. "When you're in touch with the earth, it brings you peace of mind," says Anstace.

Both are well-known for their weekly television show *From A Country Garden* which has been on PBS for seven years now. Filmed right in their own garden, Larry in his familiar floppy hat and Anstace in her overalls dispense practical, expert advice on landscaping, growing flowers and vegetables, and even cooking and preserving.

In their various media endeavours as in the garden, the two complement each other. Anstace's writing, which includes a myriad of magazine articles as well as her 1981 book *Vegetable Gardening*, is usually accompanied by photos and graphics by Larry. On television and radio as in real life, Anstace plays straight man to Larry's dry Irish humour.

They have had a long and beneficial association with the Kemptville Horticultural Society. In the 1970s, during her term as president, Anstace was instrumental in having Arbour Day reintroduced to encourage tree planting at local schools. Both she and Larry have been involved in getting area children turned on to gardening through the society's junior program. Before the demands of the garden, the writing and the broadcasting became as great as they are today, Anstace visited schools and helped judge junior gardens. The barbecue and pool party they continue to host every summer for local junior gardening participants has become a tradition.

Hands-on gardening courses at Evergreen Farm and talks, lectures and slide shows for various groups are other ways that Larry and Anstace spread their love of growing things to others.

They have always welcomed the public to their gardens. On weekends, from spring through early fall, they make a point of greeting and talking with visitors. They are always happy to give help or advice which might make gardening easier and more enjoyable for people. "Gardening seems to attract a particularly nice sort of person," says Larry, "and it's a pleasure for us to have people come and enjoy the garden."

Larry and Anstace have long opened their gardens to special groups as well. Institutions such as the Elizabeth Bruyere Geriatric Hospital have for years been bringing bus loads of handicapped seniors for horticultural therapy. For the past few summers, they have hosted a Teddy Bear Picnic for area youngsters.

KEITH AND DICK EVANS
quiet, sincere and good-hearted

Keith and Dick Evans haven't won any formal awards for citizenship, nor do they belong to any committees or clubs dedicated to the betterment of society. Neither one moved away from the community to make his fortune in the world. They are not pillars in any church. But their honest, pleasant, giving natures have earned them the love and respect of friends and neighbours all over the community. They like people and they like life — and it shows.

Dick and Keith would fit the most discriminating definition of good neighbour. For example, Winnie Lamrock, their neighbour and former teacher, has dubbed them "grand fellows" for good reason. Since he moved next door to her in 1965, Keith has always kept her laneway and sidewalk clear of snow in winter. Dick, three doors down, keeps her grass in good trim, and both are always on call for her, day and night, if she needs a hand with anything.

In the winter, Keith turns on the heat at St. Andrew's Presbyterian Church, located between the two brothers' homes. At Christmas time, he dons his Santa suit and shakes his sleigh-bells for nursing homes, Sunday schools and other local organizations. He took care of the late Gordon Craig, and presently keeps Glenn Murray's bicycles in repair. Dick does "a bit of tractor work for the neighbours if they need it." He is rarely without his friendly smile.

Their mother, Helen Forbes, is from a long-established Newmanville-area family. When she married William James Evans in 1933, they lived at his family farm on the Hoey Road (Hwy 43) near Kelly's Corners. William's family had arrived in Oxford-on-Rideau when he was about six years old. He and Helen had five children: Marion (Crawford), Dick, Keith, Marie (deceased) and Faye (Seabrook).

Dick married Jean Curry in 1959, and two years later they moved to their present home on Water Street in Oxford Mills. Their four children — Arthur, Brent, Dennis and Jane — are grown and have left home. Since early in 1990, Dick has been manager of the Oxford-on-Rideau waste site at Oxford Mills where the courteous assistance he provides has helped the township's recycling project get off to a good start. Dick worked for ten years for the United Counties of Leeds and Grenville, ploughing snow and doing fencing and general maintenance. Before Borden closed in Kemptville, he worked there for sixteen years. He is an expert butter maker, a talent likely inherited from his grandfather, John Forbes, a cheese maker at Farmers Union. His present goal in life, he jokes, is to own one-fifth of Oxford Mills.

Keith, a bachelor, has worked for twenty-three years on the Rideau Canal locks at Merrickville. He has always lived with his parents, and since the death of his father in 1989, he has taken care of his mother. Keith remembers cutting cedar posts on Bolton Road for Sam Dillabough in the late '50s for five dollars a day. "In those days, you could put two dollars' worth of gas in a car and drive all night!" he laughs.

(* = Oxford-on-Rideau resident)

Back Row (L - R): Sid Boal, Rick Grahame, Pat Luther, Liuetenant Cameron Moorehouse, Liam Russell, Steven Cater, Pat Kinnear, Jamie Kinnear, Doug Barnett, Dan Gordon, Kevin Henry, *Rolly Allaby

Middle Row (L - R): Don Barnett, Don Powell, Garnet Crawford, Captain Rudy Finzel, Howard Wilson, Tom Blair, Gordon Turner, *Bill Kinnear, *Dennie Trodden

Front Row (L - R): Secretary-Treasurer Ed Tatarciuk, Lieutenant Kevin Graham, *Captain Harold Workman, *Chief Tim Bond, *Deputy Chief Gerald Cater, Captain Ken Hudson, *Lieutenant Jeff Crawford

Not Shown: Kevin Forbes, Kerry Harris, Derek South

FIRE-FIGHTERS
dedicated to public safety

It is a sad fact of life that those who are aware of the essential services provided by volunteer fire departments have usually learned about them through a tragedy. The Kemptville Fire Department has been in operation since 1855 and is always at the ready to put out fires and save lives.

For Tim Bond, who has spent nearly twenty years on the Kemptville force and is now in his sixth year as Fire Chief, being a volunteer fire-fighter is a family tradition. "My father, Bill, was a thirty-six-year member of the Kemptville Fire Department," he says. "It's in my blood." Tim and Deputy Chief Gerry Cater, a twenty-two-year veteran with the force, spend an average of about two hours a day on administration work in addition to their regular duty hours with the department.

The Kemptville Fire Department serves Oxford-on-Rideau, Kemptville and South Gower, and draws its thirty volunteer members from those three communities. The force has used the present Kemptville fire hall, orginally built as an armoury, for about twenty years. Before that, the fire station was located where the present Kemptville town hall is. The department now owns eight fire trucks. Six are kept at the fire hall for active duty while two older ones are in storage to be used in parades.

Volunteer fire-fighters are trained through district seminars sponsored by the Ontario Fire Marshall's Office and through ongoing sessions at the department level. The Kemptville Fire Department meets on the first Thursday of each month to go over the more theoretical aspects of training, often using videos and demonstrations. On the third Thursday, they have a hands-on working practice. Their own survival as well as that of the people they rescue leaves no margin for error. Despite the constant training and danger of the volunteer fire-fighter's position, there is a waiting-list of men who want to join the force some day.

The Kemptville Fire Department averages ten calls a month. At any given time, day or night, there are usually about eight volunteers ready to answer the fire emergency number. Whoever answers the call is responsible for setting the force in motion by getting information about the location of the fire or accident and then alerting the other fire-fighters on their pagers through the encoder at the fire hall. Fire-fighters go to the scene or the fire hall, whichever is closer, and the trucks are mobilized.

"Fires are caused by human carelessness," says Chief Tim Bond. For that reason, public education about fire prevention and safety is a constant concern of the Kemptville Fire Department. The vigilance of these men helps keep the whole community safer.

Jay and Rita Flannigan

JAY FLANNIGAN
enjoyment of life's simple pleasures

Jay Flannigan remembers a time when Irishtown was a thriving community, not just the name of a forgotten school section of bygone days. Around 1835, about fifty families, most of them Irish Roman Catholic, were granted fifty acres each in what came to be known as Irishtown. The old Irishtown school that Jay attended, now disguised as the Villa Toros Restaurant, is about the centre point of the area.

Both Jay's parents, John Flannigan and Ellen Finley, were descended from Irish families that came to Canada in the 1830s, at the time of the great famine in Ireland. Ellen Finley's mother was a Gaffney from McGovern Road, and she was also related to the Earlys; all three families were among the first settlers to the area.

The Flannigans took a more indirect route to Oxford-on-Rideau. Jay's grandfather James Flannigan first settled near Carsonby with his wife, Bridget McCullough. In the 1860s, when their son John was a child, they moved to Oxford-on-Rideau. For a while they had a farm on the north-west corner of what are now Hwy 43 and County Road 44. Then they moved to the Beach Road in Irishtown and bought a farm from James Deegan. The Deegans were another family of early settlers in Irishtown. There were three Deegan farms, side by side, that ran from Beach Road north to Bedell Road. Later, John, Jay's father, bought the most easterly farm from Tim Deegan. This is where Jay grew up and where he and his son Danny farm now. "There was a piece bought off this farm to build the (Bedell) station," recalls Jay.

Before the Flannigans arrived in Irishtown, James Deegan's farm was where the first mass had been held in the predominantly Irish Catholic community. "The priest came from Prescott in a horse and buggy," says Jay. Although it happened long before he was born, he heard the story many times as a child. The priest was able to make the journey about once a month. Eventually a parish was formed to include Irishtown as well as the French Settlement in South Gower further to the north. For a while, mass was held in a stone house on Clothier Street in downtown Kemptville. "Mass was more or less their outing for the week," explains Jay. "They'd go early and have a visit before church started." Holy Cross Church was built in 1889. "My father helped to draw the stones from the quarry across the road from here," Jay says.

Jay married Rita Carthy of Arnprior in 1952. One of their four children, Danny, works with Jay on their small dairy farm. They milk about fourteen cows and ship cream. "We've been that way for years," says Jay. He admits things are more difficult these days for small farmers than in the past. "Machinery is the big item now. Most of it is geared to the large farm." Neighbours no longer get together to share work as they did in the past. Things are different socially too. Community get-togethers for sports or euchre are largely a thing of the past now.

(L - R): Jack Pinder-Moss, John Hyams, Bill Shannan

GERIATRIC BUILDERS FROM BURRITTS RAPIDS
enjoying sharing their talents with the community

Every Monday morning for about four years now, five retired gentlemen have been meeting at the Burritts Rapids Community Hall to keep the building in good repair. Jack Pinder-Moss, Don MacCraken, Chris Mills and Bill Shannan met during the building of the hall's new addition which officially opened in 1988. John Hyams joined them a year ago.

The addition has its origins in pure culture. The saga began when part of a Canadian-made film called *The Boy in Blue* was shot at Burritts Rapids. As a gesture of thanks for the co-operation it received from the community, the film company donated the sets built for the movie to the village. These provided the basic building materials for the new part of the hall.

During the building of the new addition, the men who were destined to become known as the Geriatric Builders had all volunteered their time and talents to various parts of the two-year-long project, including the roof, inner partitioning, flooring, drywall, insulation and electrical work. They were among some fifty handymen, builders and tradesmen who donated their time and skills to erect the new addition.

Jack, Don, Chris and Bill got to know one another better as the work on the new addition progressed. "We found out we had particular skills that could be applied, and we all seemed to get along so well that we just carried on," explains Don. Once the addition was up, it needed decorating, and it was obvious that the old part of the hall required some improvements as well. The Geriatric Builders, as Jack Pinder-Moss dubbed them, volunteered to take on these tasks.

Since they have been meeting, they have accomplished great things, and the hall is a monument to their skill and generosity. To cure perpetual flooding of the basement under the old part of the hall, they rebuilt the two side entrances to prevent water from entering at will. They have added shelving, replaced the bulbs in the fire exits, and installed new panelling. The complete electrical replacement they have done in the basement was followed by the installation of new windows. Outside as well as inside work falls within their self-imposed mandate. Funds for the materials for their projects are raised by the hall committee.

Monday was the most convenient day for them to meet. "When we have some emergency work to do, we meet more often," explains Don.

"We're unincorporated, ununionized and unpaid," jokes Jack. "We do any handyman's job around the place ... except plumbing."

BOB AND JOYCE GRAHAM
working hard to improve community life for all

Bob and Joyce Graham were looking for a quiet country retreat to get away from the hectic city life in 1969, and Bishops Mills fit the bill. "It was absolutely unbelievable to find such a tranquil setting only one hour's drive from the nation's capital," says Joyce. Bishops at that time lacked paved roads to join it to other communities, and there were still some houses in the vicinity without running water or electricity. The pace of life there was easy, and the Grahams looked forward to a quiet, self-sufficient existence. After Bob retired in 1975, however, they began to get actively involved in both Bishops and the township as a whole.

Joyce, a child psychologist by profession, often speaks to local groups on child development and parenting techniques. She spent three years as president of the Bishops Mills Women's Institute. This past September, as their chapter's part of the township's bicentennial celebration, she and Helen Taylor organized a Victorian Tea.

Both Grahams share a long involvement in St. Andrew's United Church, Joyce as elder and Sunday-school superintendant and Bob as steward. They are members of the Oxford-on-Rideau Historical Society. Bob's research on the diary of surveyor Jesse Pennoyer inspired a skit which the Grahams and others performed for several groups in the township during the bicentennial year.

Bob has been with the Kemptville Rotary Club since 1977. He received a Presidential Citation Award from Rotary International for exceptional work during his 1983-4 presidency of his club, and is a Paul Harris Fellow. He and Joyce have travelled a number of times to Ecuador to facilitate the setting up of a Rotary-funded Agricultural Training Centre where a library has been named after Joyce. She is a past president of the Kemptville Rotary-Anns.

In 1978, Bob became the founding president of the Oxford-on-Rideau Community Association, a group he had been instrumental in setting up. He also spent two terms, from 1978 to 1982, as deputy reeve of the township. "Politics is what opened everything up," says Bob, for as a result of his four years on township and county councils, the scope of his volunteer activities widened dramatically.

Bob was appointed by the township as its representative on the South Nation River Conservation Authority, and he has spent nine of his thirteen years of service on its executive. In 1981-82, he represented the county on the Kemptville and District Hospital Board. As a member of the Oxford-on-Rideau Township Library Board since 1978, Bob can take credit for the opening of the Oxford Mills branch of the library and the leasing of the lockmaster's house in Burritts Rapids as the site for that branch.

Most of Bob's time since 1982 has been taken up with his volunteer work as a consultant to the provincial Minister of Health. He spent six years with the Rideau Valley District Health Council, three of them as chairman, and in 1987 was elected provincial chairman of Ontario's twenty-eight district health councils.

Bob has many plaques and awards to honour the work he has done to help make Oxford-on-Rideau a better place for everyone to live.

ANNA GRIER
for home and country

Anna Grier has been the backbone of Burritts Rapids for most of her ninety-seven years. From the time she first came to the village as a child until she moved to Featherstonhaugh Manor in Kemptville in 1987, her incredible energy was a positive force in Burritts Rapids community life.

With her parents, Thomas and Etta Grier, her sister Geneva, and her brothers Harold and Albert, young Anna moved to Burritts Rapids in 1908 from Wolford Township where she was born.

In 1915, after taking a course in commercial short-hand and typing at Gowling Business College in Ottawa, Miss Grier began working at T.A. Kidd's store in Burritts Rapids as clerk and postmistress. For eight years during the 1930s, she supplemented her income by working as a free-lance journalist, covering the social and recreational doings of Burritts Rapids for local newspapers. Miss Grier retired from the store shortly after the Kidds sold it, around 1950, and she and her brother Harold started their own successful store on the main street of Burritts Rapids.

Miss Grier is the only surviving charter member of the Burritts Rapids Women's Institute, which she helped establish in 1912. Among the group's earlier projects was the installation, in 1924, of the first electric street lamps in Burritts Rapids. The ten lamps cost five dollars apiece, and the Women's Institute also paid the power costs for these for the next thirty-five years until the township took over.

Miss Grier was secretary of the branch for many years, as well as president, and was also a long-time public relations officer for the North Grenville district. In recognition of her years of service to the organization, she was made a life member of both the Federated Women's Institutes of Ontario and the Associated Country Women of the World.

Another organization in which Miss Grier took an active role was the Ladies' Orange Benevolent Association. She joined the Merrickville lodge in 1922, was instrumental in starting up the Burritts Rapids lodge in 1926 and became its first Worthy Mistress. She also acted as treasurer for many years and remained a member until 1987. In the 1940s, she served at the provincial level as Worshipful Grand Mistress of Ontario East. Later, she spent twenty-four years as the Grand Secretary of the Most Worshipful Grand Lodge of Canada, where she was secretary for all provincial and local lodges across Canada. For her efforts, she was made Honorary Past Grand Mistress.

Miss Grier was always a supportive member of the Burritts Rapids Community Hall Committee, and was particularly active during the period when substantial renovations were being done to the hall as a community project. Here, as in her work with the Anglican Church Women of Christ Church and all her other pursuits, she always worked hard for her community.

JOAN AND EARL GUMMESON
leaders in the Heart and Stroke Foundation

When Joan and Earl Gummeson make a commitment, they follow through. In recent years, they have spent a great deal of time and effort promoting fitness and good health in the community through their work with the Heart and Stroke Foundation of Ontario.

"It's been a very busy job over the last six years," admits Joan. Before that time, both she and Earl had canvassed for Heart and Stroke for several years, but that had been the extent of their involvement. After Joan was asked to help out with the Kemptville chapter in 1985 and gladly did so, it was obvious that the work agreed with her and vice versa. She soon became president of the Kemptville chapter. "I had to learn it all from square one!" She remembers reading all the manuals she could get her hands on to prepare for the new job. She learned quickly and served for three successful years as president, then spent a further year as chairperson of public education. Through pamphlets, posters, talks and demonstrations at fairs and schools, Joan made sure the public was aware of the Heart and Stroke Foundation and the disease it is fighting. "Heart disease is the number-one killer in North America," she points out. She is still a member of the public education committee.

In 1986, shortly after retiring from the air element of the Canadian Armed Forces, Earl also joined the annual Heart and Stroke fund-raising campaign. He chaired the campaign and special events committee that first year. Among the special events organized annually by the Kemptville chapter are a float in the Santa Claus parade, the late-January kick-off to the campaign every winter and the duck race held on Kemptville Creek in the spring. Earl is presently chairing the human-resources committee for both the Kemptville chapter and Ontario East, and he has just finished a project which will see that all Heart and Stroke volunteers get pins to indicate their years of service. In his spare time, Earl does woodworking and works at perfecting his home made wine. He has even taught wine making at Kemptville College.

Joan and Earl both do volunteer work at the Kemptville and District Hospital, she with the Hospital Auxiliary and he, on trumpet, accompanying Joan Miller, at birthday parties. Both volunteer at Bayfield Manor as well.

The Gummesons have lived in Oxford-on-Rideau Township for eighteen years, and both their children, Sandy and Robert, live in the township with their families as well. Sandy shares her parents' love of horses and the three often ride in local parades. Sandy and her husband, Burt Matthews, enjoy entertaining the residents of area nursing homes and members of Klub 67, a Kemptville seniors club, with demonstrations of the dogs that they breed and obedience train. Robert is a Beaver leader, and both he and his wife, Maureen, canvass for Heart and Stroke.

JASON GUNDY
good athlete, good person

There can be no doubt that eighteen-year-old Jason Gundy has a natural ability for athletics. With the help and encouragement of his parents, Tony and Sylvia Gundy, Jason has had the opportunity to try and enjoy all kinds of team and individual sports. He has not only proven himself a top athlete in certain areas, but he also makes a point of donating time to help make sports more enjoyable for others.

As a child, Jason started his sports career with hockey when he was about six. Soccer, baseball and downhill skiing followed. Jason enjoyed and excelled at every sport he tried. "I've always believed you should try your hardest," he says. As a result of his efforts and his positive attitude, he was honoured as top boy athlete at the age of eleven when he graduated from Oxford-on-Rideau school.

As a teenager, Jason narrowed down his participation in community sports to hockey and baseball, adding football as well in his final year at high school where he played full back with the school team. His kicking and scoring ability won him the honour of being named CJOH athlete of the week in October 1991. In hockey, he has progressed to the Junior B level, playing defense for the Kemptville 73s. Wilfred Laurier University has invited him to try out for its hockey team.

In the summer months, baseball is where Jason really shines. In 1990, he was on the Kemptville Royals' midget-level team. However, the team entered the senior-level Eastern Ontario Fastball League, with the idea that they would improve when confronted with better pitching. The theory proved to be a sound one. Jason, with a .355 average, was one of the top-ten batters in the league, and he was selected when an all-star team was formed from the league in August 1990. During one game against the formidable Carp Valley Pride, he batted 1.000. In 1991, with no junior-level team in the Kemptville area, Jason joined the Rideau Valley Pioneers and was soon batting second in the Ontario Senior Fastball League.

Jason has known since he was twelve or thirteen that sports will play a major role in whatever he ends up doing with his life. "If I can't do it at a professional level, I'd like to teach it," he says. His present plan is to study physical education at university, then go to teacher's college to become a gym teacher like his father.

Jason realizes that reaching his present level of achievement would have been impossible without the volunteer efforts of coaches, umpires and referees at the community level. In 1991, he coached the Kemptville Royals' girls' midget team, a job he admits is more fun than work for him. Jason has also coached intramural teams at St. Mark's High School, and he referees in the winter for the Oxford Millers and the Kemptville Minor Hockey Association. Here, as in the sports he plays, he is guided by a time-honoured philosophy. "Do your best," he advises. "But if you don't have fun, there's no sense in being involved."

CHARLES HARRIS
working with others towards progress in the township

Like his father before him, Charles Harris was born and grew up on the Bedell Road farm now owned by the Maturas. The farm was originally a Crown grant to Captain John Jones in 1796. John Harris, Charles' great-grandfather, bought the whole two hundred acres from the Jones family in 1844 for two hundred pounds. His son Thomas built the house in 1874 out of stone from a quarry right on the farm. Three other prominent buildings in Oxford Mills were also built of Harris stone around the same time: the town hall and SS No 8, both in 1875, and St. John's Anglican Church in 1879.

Thomas' son, Samuel Henry, married Ida Percival in 1900. They had three daughters — Alberta, Gertrude and Irene — and one son, Charles, who was born in 1907. In the summer months, the Harrises used to ship milk from their mixed farm to the cheese factory in Oxford Mills. During the winter, they separated the cream and Ida made butter for a number of regular customers. Young Charles used to turn the churn for her and she showed him how much salt to put in. He listened well, for when she was on a visit to Iowa for a few weeks, he was able to keep the customers supplied. "I made the butter and they never knew the difference!" he recalls.

Charles married Dorothy Wilcox from Eganville in 1937. Dorothy taught at SS No 8 in Oxford Mills before they were married; her sister Marietta took over the school at that point because married women were not allowed to teach in those days.

Also in 1937, Charles began his long career as a school trustee on the board of his old school,

SS No 8. Back then, each school section had its own trustees, and Charles was chairman of SS No 8 until 1946, when a township board was set up. He was chairman again from 1957 to 1964. In 1967, Oxford-on-Rideau amalgamated with Kemptville and South Gower to form a single school board of five trustees. Charles was elected chairman of that board and held the position for two more years. "I quit when they went into the county board," he says. Like many others at the time, he felt that combining Leeds and Grenville into a single board was not in the taxpayers' best interest.

"In the '50s and early '60s we were having trouble getting teachers to go into those small schools," he says. After three of the township's many one-room schools were condemned by the Department of Health, a new twelve-room school was opened in Oxford Mills in 1964, and the smaller schools were closed.

In 1947, Charles was one of fourteen dairy farmers in the Kemptville area who got together and borrowed money to start up the Eastern Ontario Cattle Breeding Association, which later became known as Eastern Breeders Inc. His involvement with the successful organization continued until he dispersed his own pure-bred Holstein herd, Harrishome.

Neither Dick nor Ann, Charles and Dorothy's two children, wished to farm, and in 1972, Charles sold the farm. "I had to retire," he says. He and Dorothy reserved a corner of the farm where they built themselves a new home. Dorothy passed away in 1984.

Back Row (L - R): Lillian Leonard, Joyce Madill, Barbara Kelemen, Ann Morey, Marg Brioux
Front Row (L - R): Jeanne Young, Deedie Mehlman, Teresa Harrison, Virginia Daoust, Cathi Finley, Maureen Kane
Not Shown: Fran Brauneisen, Helen Donaldson, Nancy Headrick, Youvapa Herda, Heather Howard, Carole Jansen,
Liz Kay, Jeanne Mikkelborg, Maureen Rose, Carolyn Wellstein, Gail Wheeler, Susan Willis

HOLY CROSS PARENT VOLUNTEERS
caring people who make things happen

At Holy Cross School, the efforts of a small group of parent volunteers are helping all the students get the most out of their education. By making a regular commitment of their time and talents to the school, these parents give the teachers more time to use their special expertise with the children. Mary McClory and Cathy Empey, both grade-two teachers and, for the last three years, the volunteer co-ordinators for the school, are in agreement about the parent volunteers: "They're excellent!"

Parents normally do not work with their own child's teacher at Holy Cross. Rather, they are assigned to another class-room where a teacher is in need of some assistance. They may be asked to work with small groups of children to read, drill words, help with math or go to the library. The teacher may need them to work one-on-one with children on computers or in reading conferences; helping children practise motor skills and hand-eye co-ordination are other tasks the parents may be asked to do.

Volunteers help the half-time librarian keep the school library running smoothly by keeping track of borrowed books, updating the card catalogue and making the library materials familiar and accessible to the pupils. They also assist with the bi-weekly hot-dog program. And parents do yard duty at noon hours to give the teachers time to unwind and enjoy their lunch.

Class trips are a time when even occasional volunteers are able to help out to make groups of students small and manageable. The Holy Cross kids go on a wide variety of cultural and field trips each year, and parent volunteers are an essential part of these trips that have included the National Arts Centre and the aviation museum. In June the grade-8 students were able to go to Toronto for a two-day jaunt because parents were willing to accompany them. Parents are also indispensable at track meets and other athletic events where they help out and give encouragement to the competitors from Holy Cross.

The children at Holy Cross are given the opportunity to get first-hand information from some parents about their jobs and interests. One day, grandparents were invited in to talk about their own school-days.

All the children in the school win when parents like these volunteer their time.

*Back Row (L - R):   Michael Johnson, Wendy Van Lanen, Leslie Stewart,
Denise Arcand, Scott Hossie*
Middle Row (L - R): Kirsten Kuilder, Jillian Brazil, Beth Morey, Karen Willis
Front Row (L - R): Matthew Vandongen, Paul Hossie, Ryan McKenzie

HOLY CROSS STUDENTS
community leaders in the making

Holy Cross School boasts a number of young Oxford-on-Rideau residents who have been giving up some of their spare time to help make life better for others in the community.

Denise Arcand, Jillian Brazil, Beth Morey, Leslie Stewart, Wendy van Lanen and Karen Willis joined the volunteer Candy Stripers at Kemptville and District Hospital. One or two evenings each week, the Candy Stripers assist nurses with the mainly elderly patients, passing out refreshments and snacks and chatting with the patients as well.

Mike Johnson and Kirsten Kuilder joined a group of volunteers who help out at Bayfield Manor one or two evenings a week. Like the Candy Stripers, they serve refreshments and assist the Bayfield residents where needed. Both Mike and Kirsten enjoy conversing with the elderly people.

Matthew Vandongen, Paul Hossie and Ryan McKenzie, all grade-six students, have helped give Holy Cross and its doings a higher profile in the community through their semi-monthly column Holy Cross Alive in the *Advance*. They have included information about sports, plays, competitions, events and anything else that is happening at Holy Cross. They received guidance and assistance from teachers in the fall when the techniques of gathering and writing up news were new to them. After Christmas, however, they took turns researching and writing up the column on their own. Through this well-written effort, these three have done a great service for their school and for the community.

Scott Hossie, age fourteen, was nominated by the Holy Cross staff as the school's candidate for the Catholic Youth Award, presented annually by the Ontario Separate School Trustees to an outstanding student in the province. Scott was chosen to represent Holy Cross School because of his exceptional academic record, his volunteer work in the community, his good Christian attitude and his all-round personality, says Emmett Doyle, principal of Holy Cross School. Since he was in grade four, Scott has served as an altar boy in the church. He has also participated on basketball, volleyball and track teams, and is a member of 4-H with four projects to his credit already. Holy Cross presented Scott with a certificate and plaque in recognition of his good citizenship.

For Leslie Stewart, age thirteen, the unveiling of Oxford-on-Rideau township's own official flag in May was a very special event. Out of some fifty entries from local school children in a 1990 competition held by council for new flag designs, Leslie's was chosen. "We're very proud to have Leslie as one of our students, and we're happy to see her talents as an artist being recognized," says Holy Cross Vice Principal, Bryan Kealey.

CLIFFORD AND ETHEL HUTCHINS
still laughing after 63 years of marriage

Clifford Hutchins' family has lived on Bolton Road for a long time. His grandfather, William Hutchins, came over from Scotland and built a log house on a hundred acres between Newmanville and Bishops Mills. "He worked on a boat before he came here," says Clifford. William married Jane Forbes, who had grown up next door to his new home. The Forbes family had been settled in the area for some time then.

William's mixed farm passed to the only son among his four children, William John, who married Emily Elizabeth Laflaver and had five children of his own. They all went to SS No 21, Cedar Grove school, which used to be near the corner of Bolton and Forbes Roads. Of the five, Clifford, born in 1904, inherited the farm. William John died of kidney trouble when Clifford was only seventeen, and not long afterwards, the farmhouse burned down. "We had it almost out and the well went dry," Clifford remembers. The present house was built on the same site.

Clifford married Ethel Weir, from Lloyds Mills near Algonquin, in 1928 at the Maynard manse. They met at the farm of her sister and brother-in-law, Elsie and Lorne Render. "Lorne used to hire young lads to pick potatoes," explains Ethel. Their two children, Marguerite (McCurdy) and Roy have, between them, produced seven grandchildren and they, twelve great-grandchildren for Clifford and Ethel. Their grandson Barry

lives right next door with his wife Cheryl (McCurdy) and their two children, Amanda and Mark.

During the '30s and '40s, the Hutchins went to Nottell's store in Bishops Mills every Saturday night. "We took butter over there in prints," says Clifford. Butter sold for fourteen cents a pound then, and eggs six cents a dozen. "We used to put butter down in the summer in a big crock. Kept it in the cellar. Killed our own pork and put it down in salt in a barrel," Clifford says. They took turns with the neighbours drawing milk to the Farmers Union cheese factory, and then drew cheese from there up to Burritts Rapids to go on the boat. In the winter, when the cheese factory closed down, they separated the milk and sent the cream to the creamery in Kemptville. For over thirty years, "till I got the pension," Ethel used to take chickens and eggs to the Brockville market every Saturday. Clifford quit milking about twenty years ago. "I'm just playing around now," he laughs.

"We farmed with the horses for quite a while," says Clifford, who remembers very clearly their first tractor, an International. "I got it for $1,240, full of gas, and I drove it home from Kemptville!" Ethel was a good horsewoman. "I could handle horses good but I never drove a car," she says. "I mind one time the horses slipped on the ice at Hares Hill. I was sitting in the cutter and Theodore Beach came along and got us out."

DON AND JEAN KNAPP
pillars of the community

Even though Don and Jean Knapp stopped operating their orchard just outside Kemptville in 1986, the name Knapp is still synonymous with apples to many people. Buying a house on ten acres with a productive orchard on Hurd Street was a natural thing for Don and Jean to do in 1949. Don's degree from the Ontario Agricultural College in Guelph gave him the know-how; Jean certainly knew the area and the people who lived there because she had grown up on the farm right across the road. "I missed the people but not the work," says Jean, looking back at when they finally cut down the trees. "There's a lot more work to producing an apple than the public realizes."

Jean's parents, Harry and Christina Earle, bought their eighty- acre farm on the east side of Hurd Street when Jean was just a baby. Mrs. Earle, now ninety-eight, lives at Bayfield Manor. Don is the great-grandson of Sam Jakes in Merrickville. In fact, the 1861 building which was expanded into the inn was in the Jakes family until it was sold around 1930. Don's mother, Laura Jakes, grew up there. The family of his father, Clifford Knapp, had lived for some time in Oxford-on-Rideau before moving to Merrickville where Don spent his youth. Sam Jakes used to have a general store called the Jakes Block. All the items most people needed in their daily lives, including groceries, clothing and hardware, were available on four levels. You could take the yard goods you bought on the first floor directly up to the tailors on the third floor. There was even an elevator.

Don worked at Kemptville College from 1949 till his retirement in 1981. Jean did most of the work for the apple business while she was home raising their two daughters, Heather and Sandra. Both Don and Jean have been associated with St. John's United Church since their marriage in 1946. Don has been chairman of the board there in the past. Although Jean is not formally a member of the United Church Women or the Kemptville District Hospital Auxiliary, she gives assistance to those groups whenever it is needed. "My part isn't that great," she says. "I just help where I can." She also drives for Meals on Wheels through Kemptville Home Support. Before Kemptville District Hospital was built in 1960, Don was involved in some of the fund-raising activities. In the 1970s, he spent a few years on the hospital board.

The Rotary Club has been a major commitment in Don's life since he joined in 1960. He has held a number of offices with the local chapter, including president, and has also chaired committees as diverse as Christmas tree sales and membership. Now, as club historian, he is responsible for preparing the scrap-book with newspaper clippings of Rotary activites which will be presented to the outgoing president. Jean joined the Rotary-Anns when the group was formed in 1970 and has been president as well as convener of some committees.

KATHY & ASHLEY KNOTT
willing hands to help others

Kathy Knott has never been one to sit around waiting for others to get things done. When she isn't actually initiating something, she's usually pitching in, helping. Not just Burritts Rapids, where she and her family have lived for twelve years, but the entire township has reaped the benefits of her community work.

For five years, Kathy has been chairperson of the Oxford-on-Rideau Recreation Committee, a rather loosely structured body whose mandate is to set up and oversee township-based activities for young and old alike. Kathy co-ordinates all the various recreational endeavours across the township and is always on the lookout for grants so that residents can have a variety of activities to choose from. Current township offerings include gymnastics, T-ball and softball.

Kathy is also an active member of the Burritts Rapids Community Hall Corporation. She has been chairperson more than once and for the last two years has served as secretary. The hall corporation's three main annual fund raisers are all meals served in the hall: a turkey dinner in the fall, Italian night in February and a pancake brunch in the spring. Kathy always helps out on these occasions by setting up and cleaning up the hall and by cooking, baking and serving food.

Kathy was always an active member of Story Hour, the Burritts Rapids weekly play group held in the old hall basement for mothers and preschoolers. And for several years, in the village hall, she led evening aerobics classes to help keep area women fit.

Following in her mother's footsteps is nine-year-old Ashley. A grade-four student at Merrickville School, Ashley has been helping out at community suppers and teas for a number of years already. She takes guests' orders, serves their food and cleans up afterwards. Bimonthly bingos were held at the hall until recently, and Ashley was always on hand to help sell 50/50 tickets, count cards, pass out coffee and take care of the money when others were busy.

On other occasions, Ashley has contributed to the Burritts Rapids community by blowing up balloons and helping with the preparation of box lunches for the annual village picnic. Her help has been invaluable to her mother in carrying supplies from their home to the hall.

WINNIE LAMROCK
a respected educator

One of the most respected residents of Oxford Mills is Miss Winnie Lamrock. "I was a teacher for forty-one years and six months," she remembers fondly. Now, at the age of eighty-seven, a quarter century after her retirement from teaching, she is as interested in children as ever and enjoys her weekly contact with the nursery at St. Andrew's Presbyterian Church.

Miss Lamrock's great-grandfather, William John Lamrock, came to Oxford-on-Rideau Township before 1841 and settled on the 10th line. The house he built is still there. In 1878, his son John Abram, Miss Lamrock's grandfather, built a red brick house on a hundred acres just north of Oxford Mills, on the road to Actons Corners. That house can also be seen today. John Abram and later his son John Edward operated a mixed farm. In 1902, John Edward married Maggie Florilla Patton, who had taught school until she was married. They had two daughters, Winnifred May in 1904 and Katie Eleanor four years later.

Winnie went to SS No 8, the two-room school in Oxford Mills which presently houses a branch of the Oxford-on-Rideau Public Library. After that, she attended Kemptville High School where, she recalls, she liked English, history and chemistry but not physics. Then she went away to Ottawa to normal school for a year to get her teacher's licence.

Winnie's first teaching job was in the the same place her mother had taught, the junior room of her old school, SS No 8 in Oxford Mills. For three years, she taught grades one to four to about thirty children at a time. The next seventeen years were spent teaching in Lanark County. She then returned to the Oxford Mills school where, at one point, she was teaching forty-two children from grade one to grade eight. In 1964, she moved to the large new school in Oxford Mills that replaced the small schools in the township. Two years later she retired.

When she returned from Lanark County in the mid-'40s, Miss Lamrock lived with her parents and sister. After the deaths of their father (1955) and mother (1958), the Lamrock sisters sold the farm and bought the house on Water Street in Oxford Mills where Miss Lamrock lives today. Katie kept house for them until her death in February, 1988.

Miss Lamrock is a long-time member and supporter of St. Andrew's Presbyterian Church in Oxford Mills. She taught Sunday school there for many years and used to be an industrious member of the Ladies Aid. "I'm glad we have young people for the Sunday school and Ladies Aid now," she says. She still helps out in the kitchen at church functions and keeps track of the birthdays of the Sunday school children.

Now a life member of the Women's Institute, Miss Lamrock joined the Oxford Mills branch in 1947. She has served as both curator and assistant curator of the Tweedsmuir History, the record of local history kept by each branch of the Women's Institute.

(L to R): Lara Witham, Mahnaz Rahman, Courtney Holmes

LIBRARY VOLUNTEERS
always competent and reliable

The Oxford-on-Rideau Public Library has two locations, Oxford Mills and Burritts Rapids, for the convenience of township residents. At each branch, the job of the regular librarian is made easier by volunteer assistants. To date, both locations are open Tuesday afternoons, Wednesday evenings and Saturdays for a total of ten hours a week.

"A small community library like this relies very heavily on the co-operation and support of the people who use it," explains Olivia Mills, librarian of the Burritts Rapids branch. She really appreciates the assistance of four regular volunteers. "Other people are always willing to help out if there's something to be done," she adds.

Vernie Foy and Aileen Weston have been coming in to the Burritts Rapids branch most Tuesdays and some Saturdays for several years. "They can do everything," says Olivia, who admires the way the two women work together. Manning the desk, keeping the shelves in order, repairing books, filing — there is no aspect of the librarian's job these two do not do well. Olivia also appreciates the suggestions they make from time to time to help make the library more efficient; the perspective they give her helps her make decisions more easily, she says. Vernie and Aileen can and do run the library in Olivia's absence. "I can leave them in the library in complete confidence," says Olivia. "That's the beauty of people who work well."

Both branches have seen a surge of younger volunteers in the last year. Courtney Holmes, now eleven, began helping out on Wednesdays and Saturdays at the Burritts Rapids branch in the winter of 1990, and eleven-year-old Amanda Watkins joined her there on Saturdays a year later. Mahnaz Rahman, eleven, and Lara Witham, ten, volunteered their services in November, 1990, to former Oxford Mills librarian Lynne Heath. They have been helping out at that branch every free moment they have ever since.

The four girls assist the librarians by putting away returned books, stamping out newly borrowed books, cataloguing new books, straightening up the books in the shelves and doing minor repairs on damaged books. Courtney, Amanda and Lara like working on the desk the best, while Mahnaz' favorite activity is typing out new catalogue cards.

Gertrude Pettapiece, Eva MacMartin, Lillie Patterson

EVA MACMARTIN, LILLIE PATTERSON AND GERTRUDE PETTAPIECE
a wealth of shared memories

The Francis sisters — Eva MacMartin, Lillie Patterson and Gertrude Pettapiece — are in their nineties now and residents of Hilltop Nursing Home in Merrickville, but they will always be considered a part of the Oxford Mills community which was their home for most of their lives.

Their parents were Samuel Francis, born in the vicinity of Mountain, and Mary Grier of Heckston. They were married at Shanly in 1892, and were living at Heckston in 1894 when Eva was born. Three years later, Lillie came along, and by 1900, when Gertrude was born, the family was living in Oxford-on-Rideau Township, on the Hoey Road about a mile west of Actons Corners on a farm now owned by the Armstrongs. The three sisters went to SS No 6, Actons Corners school, until 1910 when the family moved to the stone house now occupied by Towers on Craig Road. The girls switched to Todd's School then. "We all tried the (high school) entrance from there," recalls Mrs. Pettapiece, although none went on.

In 1920, Lillie married James Patterson, whose family had lived in the Oxford Mills area for several generations. With their only child, Harold, they lived on various farms around Oxford Mills, eventually buying the post-office building on Water Street in Oxford Mills. The family moved in and James ran the post office till his death in 1950. Lillie took over as postmistress, and when she retired in

1961, the post office moved to the home of Joyce and Maurice Seguin. Lillie lived in the former post office until it burned in 1966. From then until she moved to Hilltop in 1984, she lived in a house across the street that she bought from Harold and his wife Bernie. She has one grandson and two great-granddaughters.

Eva married John MacMartin in 1921. John grew up where the Willis Hamiltons now farm. His father was Joseph MacMartin and his mother, Lydia Merrick. Eva and John bought the farm on Craig Road from Samuel Francis, and there they raised their two sons, Arnold and Malcolm. While John farmed, he drew the mail as well. In 1964, they moved to Main Street in the village of Oxford Mills, and ten years later John gave up his mail route. After John died in September 1986, Eva moved first to Brookview Manor then to Hilltop. She now has five grandchildren and six great-grandchildren.

When Gertrude married Henry Pettapiece in 1924, the couple moved into his family home on County Road 18 where Doug Dennison lives now. Like her sisters, Gertrude was married in St. John's Anglican Church in Oxford Mills. She occasionally played the piano there for special occasions. "I taught myself," she says. Eventually, she and Henry moved to Merrickville where Henry died in 1972. They had no children. Gertrude moved to Hilltop in 1990.

RAY AND LOIS MacNILAGE
preserving roots through music

Ray and Lois MacNilage spend a lot of time these days making life more fun for seniors in local nursing homes.

"I think it's well worth anyone's while to do it," says Lois, who enjoys her weekly trip to Bayfield Manor to pass out refreshments and help residents with their exercises. She also gives time on a regular basis to the Seniors Support Centre in Kemptville, serving dinner and providing transportation for medical appointments and shopping trips.

Ray is a volunteer for the Cancer Society, driving patients to Ottawa clinics. But he's best known in the area for his musical group, the Town and Country Band. "We play for fun at hospitals, seniors' homes, picnics, family reunions, whatever," he explains. They never charge for these performances. "This is just for the good of the people," explains Ray.

Ray began his lifelong career as a performing musician at Adam's School when he was about twelve. His Uncle Melvin had recently taught him to play the violin, and Ray made his debut at a school concert. "That sort of got me started," he recalls. As a teenager, he belonged to a group that played old-time country music. John O'Neill, another township resident, played guitar and violin with that group. "We played for dances all the time," says Ray.

Ever since then, Ray has been with one group or another, playing country, old-time and blue grass. Since Gary Tousaw recently joined Ray's group, the Town and Country Band have added gospel to their repertoire.

Ray is a descendant of the Adams family, one of the earliest families to settle in Oxford-on-Rideau Township. The Adams farm near Millars Corners became the MacNilage farm when Ray's grandmother, Margaret Adams, married Ben MacNilage. Their son Basil and his wife, Annie Ogilvie from South Mountain, carried on the farm and eventually it came to Ray, their only son.

In 1955, Ray married Lois Hutchins, whose family also goes back several generations in Oxford-on-Rideau. Lois went to Brown's School, which used to be on County Road 18 near Jig Street. The two farmed till 1966, then moved closer to Kemptville where Ray was employed at Kemptville College till his retirement in 1988.

Ray and Lois are both members of St. John's United Church in Kemptville. She is on the board there and is also the leader of one of St. John's four United Church Women units. In 1992, she will become the overall president of all four units. Lois recently joined the Vimy Rebekah Lodge in Kemptville.

The MacNilages enjoy meeting and helping people. "It's like anything," explains Ray. "You have to like it."

DICK McFADDEN
a neighbor for all seasons

When Dick McFadden retired from the Rideau Correctional Centre in 1979 after working there for thirty-one years, he was presented with a carved penholder inscribed with the following message: "For a Guy that Helps Everybody." This echoes the reputation he has around Burritts Rapids.

For over forty years, in his spare time, Dick has been a general Mr. Fixit, helping friends and neighbours keep their farming and gardening machinery in good running condition. After taking a welding course in Smiths Falls during the '50s, Dick bought a welder which he has used ever since to repair tractors, balers, combines — "more or less anything that would break on a farm," he explains. Any charge he made for his work was only to cover the cost of materials, never his labour.

From the age of one, Dick has lived on a seventeen-acre farm just west of Burritts Rapids. His father, Hugh, began farming, and his mother, Sarah Ellen, carried on after Hugh's death in 1927. Dick remembers that while he and his sisters, Hazel and Mabel, were growing up during the Depression, his mother traded butter and eggs from their farm for sugar, flour and other staples at Kidd's store in the village. Dick still keeps a few beef cattle on the beautiful riverside farm as a hobby.

After spending four and a half years overseas during World War II, in both anti-aircraft and service corps, Dick returned to Burritts Rapids. He and Nell, whom he had recently married, settled down on the family farm and got involved with the community.

About thirty-five years ago, Dick was a member of the hall committee in Burritts Rapids. Things were a lot different then, he recalls. For one thing, committee members were appointed or invited, not elected as they are now. For a while, Dick acted as hall caretaker; keeping the place warm with wood-burning heaters was quite a task. Before World War II, he flooded the village rink and cleared the snow from it with a team of horses. When his son David was young, Dick and a few other parents started an outdoor rink behind the hall for village kids to use, and kept it going for a couple of winters.

These days, Dick is very active in the Burritts Rapids New Horizons Club, a social and recreational organization for seniors funded by a government grant. He is now a member of the executive of this busy group which offers potluck suppers, card games and activities such as carpet bowling to the large number of seniors in the area.

NOTE: It was a great loss to the Burritts Rapids community and to the McFadden family when Dick passed away on September 2, 1991.

IAN McLAUGHLIN
committed to community service

Ian McLaughlin doesn't need volunteer work to fill up his spare time, but the busy horticulturalist makes a point of donating some of his talents and energy to several organizations which serve the community.

"I respect all the service organizations," says Ian, who is a charter member of the Kemptville Kinsmen Club. In his twenty years with the club, he has been president twice and has filled all other positions on the executive except treasurer. He has also chaired most of the major Kinsmen community projects: semi-annual blood donor clinics, the spring fair, the Santa Claus parade and the skating rink on the Kemptville Creek. Beyond the club level, Ian has been zone deputy governor over five zones and was district governor of Northern and Eastern Ontario and Quebec.

Ian is in his twelfth and final year on the Kemptville District Hospital Board, and is now the board's chairman. Each of the twenty members on the board acts as a liaison between the hospital and the public that he or she represents. "We're there to balance services against the dollars," Ian explains. The board recently eliminated obstetrics from the hospital. "We had to make a decision that none of us liked to make," says Ian.

When Ian makes up his mind to support an organization or cause, he makes a whole-hearted commitment. The Heart and Stroke Foundation is a good example. He accepted an invitation to take part in the annual fund-raising campaign in 1987, and within a few months he was into a two-year term as president of the local chapter. Ian spent another year as chairman of the February campaign, and since then has been regional board president, linking the provincial Heart and Stroke board with the twenty local chapters in Eastern Ontario. In this capacity, he meets with similar representatives from across Ontario four times a year to share fund-raising ideas. Kemptville's annual duck race is a successful and unique idea that originated in Alberta and spread to other places through this board.

The North Grenville District Association for the Mentally Handicapped is another organization that has benefitted from Ian's commitment and abilities. Since he joined in 1981, the association has raised the money to put up the ARC Industries building on Hwy 43. Once the building was up, a board of directors was recruited to handle its day-to-day operation as well as that of three group homes in the area. Ian finished three years as chairman in 1989, and is still a member of the board.

"There are a lot of people out there who are willing to volunteer," says Ian. "They're just waiting to be asked."

STELLA MANEILLY
a respected lady of Bishops Mills

Stella Maneilly, at age ninety, is considered by many to be the matriarch of Bishops Mills. Although she was born and spent her childhood at Snowdon's Corners in Wolford Township, she has lived in or near Bishops Mills since she married Harvey Maneilly on June 2, 1920.

The Maneilly family farm on Limerick Road was first settled by Harvey's father, David, who came out from Ireland. When Harvey married Stella Snowdon, his father lived with the young couple at the farm. Her father-in-law was a real Irishman, recalls Mrs. Maneilly, and spoke with a thick brogue. "It took me a little while to get used to him!"

The church has always been important in Mrs. Maneilly's life. At Snowdon's Corners during her childhood, she attended Mount Zion Methodist Church. In Bishops Mills, she continued her association with the Methodist church, which later became known as the United Church. For many years, she sang in the choir. A long-time member of the United Church Women, Mrs. Maneilly still does cooking for church events. Although she no longer does knitting, crocheting and other fancy work, she still helps out with quilt making. Until recently, she also helped out at socials. She continues to be a highly respected member of both the church and the community. On occasion, although she has never joined the Women's Institute, she attends meetings of the Bishops Mills chapter which meets in the Temperance Hall directly across the road from her home.

Five years ago, when Mrs. Flora Hamblyn moved from Bishops Mills to Brockville, Mrs. Maneilly took over the job of writing up the social doings of Bishops Mills folk for the Kemptville *Advance* and the Prescott *Journal*. She depends on people to call her and let her know what they're up to for her column, as she doesn't get out and about as much as she used to.

Mrs. Maneilly sold the Limerick Road farm in 1967 when her husband died, and moved into the village house where she resides today. In the more than seventy years she has lived in the area, Bishops Mills has changed and become more up to date, although the community is still friendly and closely knit. For the first five or six years she and Harvey were married, they didn't have a car. "I can remember driving the horse and buggy to the blacksmith shop to have the horse shod," she says. The blacksmith shop used to be on the corner across from the present store. It is long gone, as is the cheese factory that blew up in the 1920s, and the sawmill that was located just down the road from where she lives now. What is now the Pentecostal Church used to be known as the Holiness Movement.

Harvey and Stella had two sons, Russell and Harry, and acted as foster parents for several years to three boys, one of whom, Edwin, they adopted. Today Mrs. Maneilly has six grandchildren and eight great-grandchildren.

OLIVIA MILLS
'doing nothing' a foreign concept

In the twenty-two years she and husband Chris have lived across from the community hall in Burritts Rapids, Olivia Mills has managed to make a very positive impact on the village. "I like children," she says, and much of the community-oriented work she has done has been for the benefit of young people. As librarian of the Burritts Rapids branch of the Oxford-on-Rideau Public Library for the past three years, she has been holding a special morning story time for preschoolers, outside the library's regular hours.

When her own children were growing up, Olivia spent eighteen years volunteering in all local levels of the Girl Guide movement. As a child she was a Girl Guide and later a Guider in the United Kingdom. In 1975, to accommodate the large number of little girls living in and around Burritts Rapids whose parents had to transport them to Oxford Mills or Merrickville each week for Brownies, she joined with Liz Smith to start up a local pack. Olivia went on to give strong and inspiring leadership to groups of Guides and Pathfinders.

Olivia was a member of the Women's Institute when Burritts Rapids had its own chapter, and through it she began her seven-year involvement with 4-H as a leader. As with everything she puts her hand to, she immersed herself in the experience. "I quite enjoyed that," she says of the many new skills, such as bread making and quilting, that she learned during her association with 4-H.

Both she and Chris have been staunch members of Christ Church in Burritts Rapids, serving on committees and organizing and taking part in activities.

Olivia learned to love gardening from her father in Ireland. In addition to contributing to the horticultural beauty of the village over the years with her own home garden, she assisted Renee Smith, in June 1991, in organizing a tour of area gardens. Proceeds from the popular tour went toward maintenance of the Burritts Rapids community hall.

As a current member of the Architectural Conservancy of Ontario Inc. and past member of the Merrickville Historical Society, Olivia is intensely interested in encouraging people to preserve their local heritage. In fact, she was initially attracted to the Women's Institute by the meticulous detail in the community records kept in their Tweedsmuir History. As her contribution to the historical theme of Oxford-on-Rideau's bicentennial, Olivia put together a history of the two branches of the Oxford-on-Rideau Public Library.

ETHEL AND GRENVILLE MOFFITT
politically-minded and community-oriented

Ethel Moffitt has lived most of her life in the Actons Corners community on Hwy 43. The highway was known as the Hoey Road when she was Ethel Evans, a student at SS No 6, Actons Corners school. Ethel's family is an old one in the area. Her great-grandmother, born in Ontario in 1835, gave birth to Ethel's maternal grandfather, Robert Weir, in Oxford-on-Rideau Township.

In 1935, eighteen-year-old Grenville Moffitt, who had been born in Kars, moved to a farm on the Hoey Road with his family. The Moffitts had lived in Millars Corners for a few years prior to moving to Actons Corners. Grenville was a corporal during his six years in the army. During World War II, he was stationed at No 1 Proving Grounds, Ottawa, as well as in Kingston. Ethel joined him when they were married in 1942. In 1946, after Grenville's discharge from the army, the couple bought the farm where they still live. The absence of a house was an easy problem to solve: they bought a house in Smiths Falls and had it dismantled and moved to the farm with the help of their neighbours.

Grenville worked as an electrician in Smiths Falls from 1955 to 1975. They farmed at the same time, milking about a dozen Holsteins. While their five children — Gary, Ron, Ian, Marlyn (Hicks) and Connie (McNamee) —

were growing up, Ethel helped keep the farming operation going.

Both Ethel and Grenville are interested in politics. Ethel is the Progressive Conservative municipal chairperson for Oxford-on-Rideau Township and works hard on behalf of the party. Grenville was a councillor in Oxford-on-Rideau for eleven years beginning in January 1975. During his service, land-severance laws changed radically. "It took a lot of extra hours to get that settled," he recalls. The minimum lot size was reduced to one acre outside hamlet areas, and building began to increase sharply in the township.

When the United Church in Actons Corners closed in the 1960s, Ethel and Grenville switched to Oxford Mills United. Grenville was on the board of stewards for many years. Ethel has been on session and, during her long involvement with the United Church Women, has been president more than once.

In 1988, Ethel joined the Oxford Mills branch of the Women's Institute where she is presently secretary. And after the Actons Corners school was closed in 1964, Ethel was instrumental in keeping the building as a community hall. She herself has been secretary-treasurer of the Actons Corners Community Association ever since.

ALICE MORRISON
an inspiring lady

One of the first things you notice when you meet Alice Morrison, now ninety-four years old and enjoying life at Bayfield Manor Retirement Home, is the sharp mind and flashing spirit that kept generations of children in line. Mrs. Morrison has spent a good part of her life teaching in one-room schoolhouses.

Born Alice Gardner at Oxford Station on August 19, 1897, Mrs. Morrison had two brothers: Mansell, a farmer, who died in 1937, and Percy, who, until his death in 1956, was the Oxford-on-Rideau township clerk.

Mrs. Morrison completed her teacher training courses at the Ottawa normal school in 1918, and spent the next seventeen years teaching in one-room public schools at Oxford Station, the Boyne near Winchester, Limebank near Manotick, and Roebuck.

"In 1935 I was married and went to Bishops Mills," says Mrs. Morrison. Her husband, Wilfrid Morrison, had the first farm east of the Bishops Mills store on what is now County Road 18 to Oxford Mills. She figured her teaching career was finished, but in 1942 she was approached to take Brown's School, located on the road between Bishops and Oxford Mills at the corner of Jig Street. It is no longer there. Mrs. Morrison spent two years there and then went into retirement again — or so she thought.

"They couldn't get teachers," she recalls. She was enticed back to Brown's School in 1947 for two more years. Her salary then was about $600 a year, paid in monthly installments. Typically she would have around thirty pupils from grade one to eight in a single class.

"Then in 1948 I went to teach in Bishops Mills," says Mrs. Morrison, who by then realized that she could not possibly retire at a time when teachers were in such short supply. She remained as the teacher in Bishops until 1961. When she started this job, the Bishops Mills school was located where the Pentecostal Church is today. It had been recently built after the old brick schoolhouse had burned down about five years previously. In April, 1950, the second school burned one night, likely as a result of being hit by lightning. The children were relocated temporarily to the Temperance Hall for the year and a half it took to build a new school on the same site as the old one. Mrs. Morrison had been retired for three years in 1964 when all the one-room schools about the township were finally closed and the pupils bused to the brand new school in Oxford Mills.

Mrs. Morrison sold the Bishops Mills farm in May of 1975 after the death of her husband, and moved to Kemptville. Up to that point, the mixed dairy 'century' farm had always been run by Morrisons. William Morrison came from Ireland and settled there in 1845. William died in 1890 and his son Jim continued to farm until his death in 1943. Wilfrid, Jim's son, carried on the Morrison farm until his own death. In 1979, Mrs. Morrison took up residence in an apartment at Bayfield Retirement Home.

GLENN MURRAY
a cheering effect on everyone he meets

Glenn Murray and his bicycle are a familiar sight to many township residents. Even in the dead of winter, whenever the skies and the roads are clear, Glenn sets out from his home at Brookview Manor to ride the byways of Oxford-on-Rideau. Glenn always has a cheerful wave for passing motorists, and his obvious contentment with life makes just about everyone who sees him feel better.

Glenn was born at Burritts Rapids in 1926, one of four children of William Murray and his wife, Geneva Grier. Glenn's sister, Isabelle (Mrs. Clifford McIntyre), and one brother, Mervin, are no longer alive, but Grenville, his other brother, lives in Kemptville.

"I went to school in Burritts Rapids a long time ago," Glenn says. His father farmed and did carpentery work as well. "He used to work at the rock cut above Deeks too," Glenn recalls. After the family moved to the Hoey Road, Glenn switched to Gibson's School at Burritt Station.

Glenn worked on the farm with his father and was often hired by other farmers to help with haying and threshing. During World War II, he didn't go overseas but his brother did. "That's when the old troop trains were running," he remembers. Glenn's father died in 1952 and his mother in the late 1970s.

"They're all at the Rapids in the family plot," says Glenn.

Since his mother died, Glenn has been living at Brookview Manor on County Road 18 near Hurd Street. Biking is his main occupation these days, although he enjoys doing jigsaw puzzles as well. He has four bicycles right now. "One of them must have thirty thousand miles on it," says Keith Evans, who keeps Glenn's bikes tuned up. Glenn easily covers three thousand miles each year in his travels.

Although he rarely goes as far afield as Bishops Mills or Millars Corners, Glenn regularly pedals to Kemptville, Pattersons Corners, Oxford Mills, East Oxford and the back roads around these hamlets. He even braves skidoo trails sometimes. He refuses to cross or ride along Hwy 43 for safety reasons. When he used to live nearer Burritts Rapids, he shunned the area south of Hwy 43 for the same reason. About four years ago, a car collided with his bicycle near Oxford Mills. Glenn was not seriously hurt, but since then he always wears an orange safety vest to make sure he is visible to traffic.

Township residents benefit from more than just the pleasant sight of Glenn going by on his bike. He also collects cans and bottles that litter the roadsides. "There's lots of them around," he explains. "I make good money!"

JEAN AND KEITH NEWANS
keen awareness of the value of heritage

If a couple could be said to have a finger on the pulse of the township, it would be Keith and Jean Newans.

Keith's great-grandfather James Newans went to Wolford township when he first came from England, but by 1856 he had settled on Bolton Road near Sanderson Road. The Farmers Union cheese factory was built on land donated from the farm in 1892 by James' son Ambrose. Shortly after that, Ambrose sold the farm to Freeman Brown and joined his father at Crozier Bridge, along the Pattersons Corners Road. Henry Newans, Keith's father, was one of the three children of Ambrose and his wife, Eliza Mercill, from Kelly's Corners. Henry married Miriam Margaret Beach, a descendent of one of the township's oldest families. When their two sons, Glen Ellwood and Keith, were young, the family moved to the farm Keith operates today at Oxford Mills. It has always been a mixed farming operation.

Keith went to SS No 8, Oxford Mills, and put in two years at Kemptville High School. He had a talent for athletics, and played hockey and softball with some of the local teams. In the early days, along with farming, Keith used his horses for a number of other jobs which included ditching roads, delivering rural mail, drawing store provisions to and from Kemptville, and taxiing village residents to various destinations. His reputation as a good story-teller is well-founded, for what he didn't manage to do first hand, he saw or heard about, and he has an excellent memory for details.

In 1960, Keith married Jean Joyner. She was born in Picton and moved to a farm on the Craig Road, known then as the Newmanville Road, in 1932. Her parents, Fred Joyner and Evelyn Donnell, were from north of Kingston. Jean went to grade ten at Todd's School, then studied for her ARCT degree in piano. After attending a summer school music course given by the Ontario Department of Education in Toronto, she began to teach music in September 1948. She regularly went to fifteen classes in thirteen schools about Oxford-on-Rideau township, later adding South Gower, Kemptville and three schools in Marlborough. After the small schools were closed in 1964, Jean was based solely at Oxford-on-Rideau school. On her retirement in 1988 after forty years of service, she was honoured as Oxford-on-Rideau's last itinerant music teacher.

Jean is an active member of the Oxford Mills community. In 1984, she started a community choir which is still a going concern today. That same year, on the occasion of Ontario's bicentennial, she produced *All Around the Township*, a history of Oxford-on-Rideau. Jean spent several years on the Oxford-on-Rideau Community Association, and through that group was instrumental in setting up the Historical Committee. In November, 1990, it became an official Historical Society, and Jean was its first president.

Keith is secretary of the Board of Stewards of the Oxford Mills United Church. "It must be forty years," he says. "I guess no one else wants the job!" Jean used to teach Sunday school and play the organ there, but is now organist at Merrickville United Church. "She went for one Sunday and stayed twenty-one years," chuckles Keith.

KARL NORENBERG
honesty and integrity in business and friendships

Ever since Karl and Christa Norenberg moved to the Kemptville area in 1964, they have proven that hard work, integrity and community involvement are a good recipe for success.

Karl's first stop in Canada after he left his native Germany in 1954 was Quebec's Eastern Townships. By 1960, he had become a director for Eastern Breeders in Brome County, and within four years, he was an assistant farm manager for the facility's headquarters in Kemptville.

Karl married Christa Kersten, who had joined him from Germany in 1962. "She was the first girl friend I ever had," says Karl. "We met in kindergarten!" After their two children, Margret and Eric, were born, the Norenberg family moved to Oxford-on-Rideau Township.

When the children were still very young, Karl gave up his position at Eastern Breeders to start his own business. Christa supported the decision even though there was an element of risk in it. She continued to work part time outside the home, adding to this and her family responsibilites all the secretarial work for the growing family business which today employs more than forty full-time people.

Despite the sixteen- and eighteen-hour days Karl and Christa often put in, they always made time for community work. In 1971, Karl was a founding member of the Kemptville Kinsmen, and in the five years he was with the club, he was involved in most of the projects going. Around the same time, he and Christa helped found the Oxford Downs Pony Club.

Karl helped out with Cubs and Scouts when Eric was younger, and Christa volunteered as a mother helper when Margret was a Brownie. She was also a parent volunteer at Holy Cross School as well as a 4-H leader. Christa has long been an active supporter of Holy Cross Church. She served on parish council for two years in the 1970s and has often been involved in church fund raising activities.

Since being invited to join the Rotary Club in 1980, Karl has been a director of the club for several years. Among the projects he has worked onis the Merrywood Camp for disabled children under the Easter Seals programme. He also participated in the International Youth Services which hosts foreign exchange students annually. The Norenbergs themselves hosted two students from Mexico and France.

Karl has been a member of the Kemptville Chamber of Commerce since its inception in 1980, and a director for five years. He has also sponsored Kemptville soccer and hockey teams for years.

For about twenty years, Karl and Christa have been sponsoring foster children in under-developed countries, through organizations such as Foster Parents Plan and World Vision. At present, they are supporting ten children from Columbia, Sierra Leone, the Philippines and India.

Both Karl and Christa Norenberg are highly respected in the community for the quiet, honest, caring approach they take to business and personal relationships.

LEO AND MARY O'NEILL
at the hub of the Pattersons Corners community

It's a toss-up whether Leo or Mary (Mayme) O'Neill's people settled in Oxford-on-Rideau first. Both the O'Neill and O'Reilly families go back a long time in the township.

Leo's great-grandfather Peter O'Neill, Esquire, came from Ireland in 1832. The first home he built on his hundred-acre farm a mile east of Pattersons Corners was a log house. The 1850 census shows that Peter's stone house was already built then, across the road from where Leo and Mary live now. According to old records, the house took two men two weeks to build. Peter's son John married Elizabeth Carmichael, who lived where Beach and Rock Roads meet today. Their son Michael and his wife, Ella Whalen, had three sons: Stanley, Leo and Willie. Stanley and his wife, Margaret, took over the original homestead, and the farm is still operated by their son Keith. Leo and Mary bought the farm across the road, which had belonged to the O'Neill family for a number of years. Willie and Helen moved into the Whalen farm on Oxford Station Road.

Mary O'Reilly's family, also of Irish origin, came to Oxford-on-Rideau from the United States while the Rideau Canal was being built. Her forefathers were mostly stone cutters who had a tradition of always calling their first-born sons Thomas. The O'Reilly farm, located on the way to Limerick from the Oxford Station Road, is still in the family; Mary's sister-in-law, Alma O'Reilly, and her son Terry farm the homestead now.

Leo and Mary both went to Pattersons Corners School as did their three children, Donald, Evelyn and Eleanor, before it was closed in 1964. "I got in the door before he got out," jokes Mary, referring to the fact that Leo is seven years her senior. Leo and Mary had a dairy operation and milked about a dozen cows. Leo worked at Sanderson Cheese in Oxford Station as a foreman from before they were married in 1943 until it closed down in 1970.

The farming years were a mixture of hard work and good times for both Leo and Mary. "We got up and milked in the morning," recalls Mary. "When Leo got home, the cows were waiting." They didn't get a milker until the 1960s. Stanley, who farmed across the road, was always there if needed. "Stanley and I worked together all our lives," says Leo of his brother who died in 1984. Finally, in 1976, Leo and Mary sold the herd and closed down the milking operation. "We had to build a milk house and at our ages it wasn't worth it!" explains Mary. Now their daughter Eleanor and her husband, Bill Hossie, raise beef at the farm.

The O'Neills have always supported Holy Cross Church in Kemptville. "We used to help with whatever there was to do — the cemetery, socials, bazaars," says Mary. Leo used to canvass local Catholic families to raise funds for the church but now, at eighty-five, he's decided to take it easy.

Front Row (L - R): Jaimie Brown, John Ferguson, Howard Leach, Hugh Craig, Bill Forbes, Tom Bingham, Grant Whisler, Don Sutton

Back Row (L - R): Doug Valcour, Doug Barnett, Kurt Poppleau, Dave McFadden, Gary Christie, Fred Robinson, Brian Clayton, Ewing Attridge (deceased), Tony Gundy, Mike Stewart

OXFORD Millers on team 1991 but not present for picture: Chalmer Conn, Ron McLean, Rick Robinson, Bob Heaphy, Ron Perkins, Bob Juneau, Gary Blake

THE OXFORD MILLERS
more than fun and sportsmanship

Don't be fooled when the Oxford Millers refer to themselves as old-timers. In hockey parlance, this simply means they are all over thirty-five! Over the hill they're not. "We're rather successful. There's no doubt about it," admits Tony Gundy, a founding member of the team.

But neither is the team a bunch of jocks looking for a little exercise and a lot of glory. What attracts members, aside from the opportunity to play competitive hockey, is good fellowship and the satisfaction of providing some support to local charities. "We try to donate about half our proceeds from tournaments to charity," explains Tony. In the past, they have given money to Kemptville District Hospital and contributed to a new Zamboni to clean their home ice at the Kemptville Community Centre.

Seven years ago, Tony and Jaimie Brown decided to organize an old-timers team just from Oxford-on-Rideau Township. The response was strong, and soon they had put together a highly competent team. To be an Oxford Miller, a player needs more than just some skill at hockey. A high value is put on co-operation and responsibility, the integral ingredients of team spirit. Would-be players are put on a waiting-list, and first become spares. When any of the eighteen regular positions open up, the spares step into them.

The philosophy of the Oxford Millers is that anything worth doing is worth doing well. They don't belong to a formal league; last year, sixteen teams played one another regularly. "It's gentlemen's hockey," explains Tony. Traditionally, their season kicks off with a tournament at the Walter Baker Centre in mid-September. However, for the last two years, they have participated in a tournament in Biddeford, Maine, at the end of July. An old-timers team from Russia was there this year. "They don't lose but they don't embarrass you unless you try to stick it to them," says Tony. Training starts in August, and the team practises on the year-round ice at the Nepean Sportsplex.

Unlike many old-timer teams, the Oxford Millers enjoy out-of-town games and often bring their families along on these occasions. In fact, the social aspect of the team is another of its drawing cards. The diversity of occupations and interests of the team members makes for stimulating conversations, and at least twice a year, the men and their wives get together for social events.

Back Row (L to R): Rachelle Poirier, Jason Valcour, Kathleen Henderson, Blake Malcomnson, Ryan Florczyk, Helen Pelletier, Courtney Holmes, Shannon Malcomnson   Third Row (L - R): Jordan Jarjour, Richard Aldham, Jessie Lindley, J.M.Seguin, Bobby Humphries, Nevin Patterson, Frank Gardell, Glen Jung
Second Rowm (L - R): Jim Hamilton, Leah Chapman, Brian Workman, Patrick Hanna, Chris Philpotts, Erin Seabrook, Kelly Johnston, Beth Simpson, Dara Manchetti, Adrienne St. Louis   Front Row (L to R): Derek Carr, Jochen Gsell, Dale Florczyk, John Thomas, Matthew Gibbon, Vicky Johnston, Glenda Annand, Zoe Childs, Shelley Workman

Back Row (L - R): Megan Graham, Cheryl Roue, Sean Deserault, Brian Dawyd, David Paterson, Kane Meikle, Braden Gray, Simon Wright, Wendy Cramp, Erin McLean   Third Row (L - R): Josh Patterson, John Aunger, Jeff Hadrovic, Chris Jung, Ben Smith, Richard McKenney, Emily Render, Nathaniel Brown, Jesse Jarjour, Jonathan Gibbon
Second Row (L - R): Shallen Seguin, Steve Patterson, Sara Clayton, Nicholas Pelletier, Christina Wright, Mandy Howard, Darren Stephenson, Jeff Hamilton, Katie Paterson   Front Row (L - R): Ashley Gray, Jason Johns, Nicholas Gray, Chris Sullivan, Jenna Lindley, Dillon Hunter, Bobby Arcand, Jennifer Goodlad, Brenna Carr Holding award: Danielle Carr and Joshua Johns

OXFORD-ON-RIDEAU SCHOOL CROSS-COUNTRY TEAM
kids helping the whole team by doing their best

Have Fun and Do Your Best is the motto of Oxford-on-Rideau School's cross-country running team. These kids have got team spirit down to a fine art and, as a team, won the Leeds and Grenville County Championship in both 1989 and 1990.

Cross-country running demands stamina that can only come from consistent practice. Starting the first week of school, any child who is willing to run every day and do his or her best can join the cross-country team; no one is ever turned away for lack of ability. Each child learns that his or her individual improvement through daily practice makes the whole team's success more likely.

At each of the four meets the team attends in the fall, boys' and girls' races are run separately for four different age groups: eight and under, nine and ten, eleven and twelve, and thirteen and fourteen. Competing schools' scores in all eight races are totalled for their overall scores. Although the Oxford-on-Rideau team is the largest in the board area for sheer numbers, it has no entrants in the oldest group because, up to now, the school has only gone to grade six. Despite being able to participate in only six of the eight possible races, the team has been able to score enough points to win the championship two years in a row. In fact, its win was based on only five races in 1989, an even more severe handicap,

because there were not enough girls in the eleven and twelve-year-old level to make a team.

When boys or girls at a given age level run a race, only the top four placed runners' scores count. However, the children all know that any time any one of them passes someone from another team, the positions of their top four runners are improved. While there are many great individual runners at Oxford-on-Rideau, the real emphasis of the team is on the group effort.

When the younger children are running, the older ones stand near the finish and cheer their team members on by name. The young ones reciprocate, and the boost it gives everyone's morale shows in the final scores. The runner who comes panting in 115th gets just as much encouragement to cross the finish as the one who is tenth. The pride each team member feels after contributing to the team's success is a unifying force in the school as a whole since nearly a quarter of the student population is involved with cross-country.

Finishing every race they start and never giving up is the theme that underlies the Oxford cross-country team members' efforts. The participation of all children from grade two up is welcomed and accepted uncritically, regardless of their natural abilities. To be a part of the team, they need only show a willingness to work as hard as they can.

Back Row (L - R): Susan Render, Brenda Gibbon, Mary Kay Walker, Chris Johnson

Middle Row (L - R): Betty Hadrovic, Gail Gray, Debbie Simpson, Cheryl Annand, Lynne Crozier, Inta Apse, Elizabeth Cramp, Gwenda Lemoine

Front Row (L - R): Vickie Patterson, Jane Holski, Linda Lee St. Louis, Donna Seguin, Lois Fitzgerald

Not Shown: Barbara Branch, Kathy Charbonneau, Joan Charlebois, Norma Davis, Rhonda Fraser, Marie Hall, Shirley Hess, Sandy Hutchins, Carolyn Jung, Roe-Anne Lindley, Faith Nelms, Betty Poirier, Molly Wolfe.

OXFORD-ON-RIDEAU SCHOOL PARENT VOLUNTEERS
making an investment in the future of the community

In years gone by, the sight of parents in a school during the day usually meant that a child was in trouble! Today, the staff of Oxford-on-Rideau welcomes parent involvement in many aspects of the educational process, particularly in kindergarten and the early grades.

While many parents have assisted their children's teachers on an occasional basis, a core group of parents has shown an ongoing commitment by helping out regularly. Some are homemakers, often with preschoolers at home. Others fit this volunteer work in around part-time and even, in some cases, full-time jobs. They are all motivated by the knowledge that providing additional hands for the more menial tasks frees up the teacher to spend more quality time with each child.

Some parents prefer to put in time at home, preparing materials for class-room activities. Especially at the kindergarten level, many of the components for arts and crafts projects need to be traced and pre-cut. Sewing costumes and book bags is another after-hours project.

Other parents assist right in the class-room, usually one morning or afternoon each week. They can work with groups of children in many ways, such as supervising painting and other art, reading stories, and helping out with class-room projects that may involve cooking, baking or modelling. Sometimes, too, parents may be asked to give personal, individual attention to particular students who may require a little extra help with reading, writing, math or other subjects. Now that simple computer programs are used regularly in kindergarten and the primary grades to help children learn to recognize letters and numbers and reinforce basic number concepts, volunteers can frequently be seen assisting children in this capacity.

Field trips are other class-room-level activities where parent assistance is always needed and appreciated. Each year, the classes in the school head out to a number of cultural events such as plays and concerts at the National Arts Centre, and outdoor sports and learning activities at places like Foley Mountain, Upper Canada Village, and Winterlude.

Certain activities benefit the whole school body and depend on parental assistance. Thanks to the hot-lunch program organized by the school committee, children can buy a lunch of soup and hot dogs one day each week. The recently organized and successful publishing house keeps up with the huge volume of books produced by the children in the school as part of the whole-language program. Special school-wide events such as concerts, field days and open houses all rely on the volunteer parents who pitch in to provide food and costumes, who help set up and take down chairs and props, and who keep score and give encouragement to young athletes.

TREVOR PELTON
a promoter of family and community

On his living-room wall, Trevor Pelton displays several awards for his contributions to the community. A plaque from the Township of Oxford-on-Rideau honours him for his twenty-eight years on council. "It went quite smoothly," he says of the period from 1954 to 1967 when he was a councillor. As deputy reeve from 1967 to 1976, he was a member of county council. He became township reeve in 1976 and held the office until 1982. As reeve, Trevor was elected Warden of the United Counties of Leeds and Grenville in 1981.

During his political career, Trevor also served for eighteen years on the executive of the Rideau Valley Conservation Authority and for several years each on the Kemptville District Hospital Board and the Merrickville and District Medical Board. For twenty-five years, he and his wife Elsie were members of the Merrickville Agricultural Society.

Another award on Trevor's wall is from the Eastern Ontario Soil and Crop Improvement Association for 1986. This certificate is awarded annually to people who have made outstanding contributions to agriculture within their community.

Rideauview Farm, on South River Road near Burritts Rapids, has been in the Pelton family for about 120 years. The stone farmhouse, now home to Trevor's son Orlin and his family, was built by Matthew Dougherty in the mid-1840s. In 1869, brothers Martin and David Pelton came from Peltons Corners in South Gower to rent the farm from Dougherty. Martin married Louisa, Matthew's daughter, and inherited the Dougherty farm on her death. Martin's second wife, Almira Watts of Andrewsville, was Trevor's grandmother.

Manson, the son of Martin and Almira, farmed with his father and later with his son Trevor who in turn farms with his two sons, Wayne and Orlin. The farm Martin inherited was mostly bush. "Between him and my father, they cleared all that's cleared," says Trevor. Rideauview was a dairy farm until a year ago. Now the Peltons raise heifers and a cash crop on about 450 acres. Most of the work land is their own. The maple-syrup operation started by Martin Pelton has continued as a family tradition. "Wayne keeps a team of horses mainly for sugar-making," says Trevor.

Trevor went to school in Burritts Rapids from 1920 to 1928. He later married Elsie Baker of Carleys Corners. Trevor and Elsie raised three children: Wayne, Orlin and Judith (McKinnon).

"We went all our lives to the United Church in Burritts Rapids till it closed in May of 1974," says Trevor, who served on session there. At that point, they had their membership transferred to St. Andrew's United Church in Bishops Mills. Elsie was a dedicated member of the United Church Women until she passed away in 1989.

JOHN POLLEY
bringing happiness to others

John Polley quit coaching kids' ball in Bishops Mills a few years ago because some of the parents disagreed with his philosophy of children's sports. "Winning is second," John insists. "Having fun is first."

In one way or another, as both consumer and provider, John has been involved in community recreation since his family moved to Bishops when he was seven. Skating was the big thing when he was a kid. "There used to be a skating rink where the ball diamond is now," he recalls fondly. "It was the only outdoor rink for miles. People used to come out from Kemptville to use it." As he and his contemporaries got older, however, interest in skating dwindled and the rink slid into oblivion for a while.

John married Irene Sztuka from the Throoptown area in 1971, and they settled in Bishops Mills. While their sons, Ben and Dan, were growing up, John and other parents about town got the rink going again. The old service building located near it burned down, and the group put up a new one with the help of a government recreation grant. Then they set up a ball diamond, and got assistance from township council to double the size of the park. "It's nice for the community," says John, who is currently co-chairman of the Bishops Mills Community Recreation Association.

In 1984, on behalf of that association, John started what is now a popular annual tradition by organizing a Hallowe'en party for local children and their parents. "That first year, we didn't expect the crowd! We ran out of prizes," he muses. Originally held in the store, the Hallowe'en party has since moved to the community hall. John gave what time he could when extensive renovations were being made to the old Temperance Hall in Bishops. "We wanted to make the hall last another fifty or sixty years," he explains.

John has turned his talent for safe driving to the community's advantage by organizing bus trips to places like Water Fun Village in the Thousand Islands and Logos Land near Cobden. Through his connections as a part-time school-bus driver, he is able to rent a bus at cost and, by charging only to cover expenses, provide groups from the Bishops area with safe, reasonably-priced transportation to fun places.

His latest contribution to township recreation took place this past July when he organized a three-pitch ball tournament for mixed teams from Oxford-on-Rideau's three major hamlets, Bishops Mills, Burritts Rapids and Oxford Mills. The winning Burritts team played the CJOH Special Effects at the end of the day. Held at the park in Bishops, the event wound up with a chicken barbecue and attracted over two hundred people from all over the area.

Now that his own kids are grown, and they can — and do — flood and clean the rink themselves, John is talking about slowing down a bit on recreation. Don't bet on it. "I have trouble saying no," he confesses, adding, "It's nice to see people happy."

GLADYS POPE
creating warmth and cosiness for the elderly

Since Gladys Pope and husband Don moved to Crozier Road from Barrhaven in 1985, she has quietly and steadily made life a little cosier for a lot of area seniors. Gladys knits and crochets lap-robes and donates them to Kemptville and District Hospital where people confined to wheelchairs take great comfort from their cheerful colours and soft warmth. In most cases, the patients become so attached to the robes that they take them with them when they leave the hospital. Gladys is kept busy meeting the demand; she recently completed her fiftieth since moving to Oxford-on-Rideau township.

Making the lap-robes would be labour of love enough, but Gladys goes a giant step further. She unravels hand-knit articles which she picks up from second-hand clothing shops and rummage sales. Then she skeins, washes and balls the wool before making the lap-robes. Friends save their wool scraps for her as well, and she has boxes of donated wool stockpiled in the garage for future projects. Gladys

remembers her mother unravelling old sweaters to make new ones during the Depression. When Gladys was a child in Shawbridge, Quebec, her grandmother taught her to knit and crochet.

When she lived closer to Ottawa, Gladys used to make lap-robes on a regular basis for the Queensway-Carleton Hospital. She also donated some to the Rideau Regional Centre in Smiths Falls. Neighborhood Services would make up bags of hand-knit clothing for her to use in her projects. "It's a very good recycling project!" she explains. "And it's something I can sit and do watching television. It keeps my hands going."

Gladys volunteers one day each week at the Salvation Army Thrift Shop in Kemptville. She has also been involved with Hey Day every year since she moved to the area. Closer to home, in Oxford Mills, she is a member of both the Women's Institute and the United Church Women.

MARGARET PORTER
pride in neighbors and community

Margaret Porter has been a valued member of the Bishops Mills community all her life. She is a Keegan, and her ancestors were among the earliest to settle in the vicinity of the village.

In 1830, Richard Keegan and his wife, Alice Darlington, came to Canada from Wexford County, Ireland. They first went to Lower Canada before settling near Bishops Mills around 1840. Their first home was below the vault of Alexander's Cemetery. Later, Richard became involved with the work of the Methodist Church as a lay preacher. "I'm told he was called Father Keegan!" says Margaret.

Robert, the oldest son of Richard and Alice, married Elizabeth Mulloy from Winchester. They built a home right across the road from the homestead. Their son, James, who later took over the farm, went to school in the winter at the stone building, in the village of Bishops Mills, that later became the Orange Hall and now belongs to the Elstones. Margaret's mother, Martha Cameron of Perth, was a schoolteacher. "She often reminded me that she taught school for $125 a year and paid her board out of that," Margaret recalls.

Margaret went to the brick school near where the Pentecostal Church is today. That school was burned in the great fire of 1942. "We lost about seven buildings in the fire," says Margaret. There was a fierce wind that April day, and the roads were impassable with spring mud. "We were on our own to fight the fire," she says of the isolated hamlet. "I think everybody has memories of it." Margaret also went to Kemptville High School.

In 1938, she married Clayton Porter from the Garretton area south of Bishops. They lived and farmed at the Keegan homestead until Clayton's death in 1948. "Clayton never saw television," Margaret points out, "and we didn't get rural hydro till 1947." Margaret farmed the homestead for another year before selling it to Clayton's brother Elwin and moving into the village with her elderly parents. It was hard to move away from the farm where she and her father had lived all their lives. "Even today I miss the farm," she admits.

The house they bought, and where she still lives, was the former Methodist parsonage. After her father died in 1950, Margaret supported herself and her mother on what she could earn as a clerk in Adams Store. "I made ten dollars a week, no side benefits," she laughs. But it got them by. After the death of her mother in 1958, Margaret worked for about twenty years at Moore Business Forms in Kemptville. Retirement has given her added time to work in her garden, one of the joys of her life.

Margaret inherited her parents' love of music. In her youth, she played piano with an instrumental quintet from South Gower Baptist Church, and she has helped out on the organ at St. Andrew's United Church in Bishops Mills for many years. Since 1980, she has been clerk of session there and is an active member of the United Church Women. "I guess because of my family background I've always tried to be useful in the church," says Margaret.

HARRY PRATT
boundless energy and enthusiasm for community service

When Harry Pratt puts on his special red suit every Christmas season, he changes appearance but not character. Harry is one of the most outgoing, active and generous residents Oxford-on-Rideau has ever had. He has lived in the area for over twenty years, and in that time has put a lot of energy, time and effort into community work. His special talent seems to lie in fund raising for charitable organizations. He doesn't see it as work, though. Harry looks upon each of his endeavours as a way to meet new people, one of his chief joys in life. "Anything I've done, I've enjoyed doing," he says. "If I didn't enjoy it, I wouldn't do it."

Harry spent twelve years on the Kemptville District Hospital Board, four and half of them as chairman. Currently, as vice-chairman of the Hospital Foundation, he is involved with fund raising for a new sun room for the hospital. He has also been active with the local Cancer Society, and has served two years each as chairman and vice- chairman.

During the ten years he was a charter member of the Kemptville Kinsmen, Harry helped out with the Santa Claus parade, the spring fair and other annual community events. The new curling rink planned for the area has also benfitted from his fund-raising skills.

As a Rotarian, Harry spent two years chairing the Ridiculous Raft Race, now an annual Canada Day tradition held at Curry Park in Kemptville. Through the Rotary Club, he and wife Sheila hosted an exchange student from Brazil this past year. Harry has helped out at the annual Fish Fry in the eight years he has belonged to the Masonic Order in Kemptville, and he is a member of the Brockville branch of the Shriners, an organization whose main mandate is the generous support of orthopedic burn units in hospitals throughout North America.

For years, Harry has supported amateur sports by sponsoring local hockey and soccer teams, and has been an active member of St. John's United Church in Kemptville.

KEN PRATT
a farmer at heart

Ken Pratt enjoyed every one of his nineteen years in municipal politics, but he admits that the last one was a bit trying. A group of residents was up in arms at the prospect of a cement plant being built at Actons Corners. They were under the mistaken impression, fuelled by wild rumours, that such an operation would involve digging and blasting. In fact, as reeve Pratt and the council tried to point out, the plant would be making slab silos, culverts and other items out of materials that would be brought in. "We stuck to our guns, us lads," says Ken. "They threatened to have us put out! But they found out later the council wasn't wrong."

Ken started as a councillor in 1957, became deputy reeve in 1965, and served as reeve from 1968 through 1976. "We didn't have the money to do what we wanted to do," observes Ken, uttering the perennial complaint of councils everywhere. As Warden of the United Counties of Leeds and Grenville for the year 1973, his job was to lead county council, a body made up of reeves and deputy reeves from all the municipalities within the two counties.

Ken is a farmer at heart. "It gets into some people's blood," he confesses. Spending three years working at Hyland Motors in Toronto during the 1930s really brought the fact home to him. "I never intended to stay in the city," he explains. "My occupation was farming, so

I came back." The farm he had grown up on at North Gower was destined to go to his brother, so in 1942, Ken bought the 150-acre farm, where he still lives, from the Wilsons on South River Road. That same year, he married Kathleen Somerville of Kemptville. Until her retirement in the late 1970s, Kathleen taught at a number of area schools, including SS No 6, Actons Corners. Their son Ronald always went to school where she was teaching at the time. Kathleen passed away in 1984.

Ken got out of dairy in 1978. "I was sixty-five then and I figured I'd better cut down," he explains. They went into beef, and now keep about fifty head. He and Ron run the farm together.

Things have changed a lot since Ken first came to Oxford-on-Rideau nearly fifty years ago. "I'm the only one at this end of the road that has any cows," he says. "When I came here first, everybody milked ten or twelve cows," he says. "We'd start threshing at one end of the road and we'd be at the other end in two weeks. Same thing for corn. Nowadays, everybody does their own work."

Ken bought his first tractor around 1948, an Allis Chalmers, ready to work, for $1400. Before that, he used work-horses, and after he bought the tractor, he still kept two of the horses. "You've got to be pretty much dedicated to be a farmer," says Ken. "And you need to be half vet to raise animals."

MABEL QUAIL
cheerful and giving to area seniors

Mabel Quail just didn't have time to experience the pleasure that volunteer work brings until she retired from the work-force in 1982. Since then, however, the Rideau River Road senior, grandmother of eighteen and great-grandmother of eighteen more, has joined several local volunteer organizations which help area seniors lead full lives. In 1989, she was presented with an Oxford-on-Rideau Township Certificate of Merit in recognition of her work with senior citizens.

Klub 67, Kemptville's senior citizens' social club, meets once a week at St. John's United Church for activities such as carpet bowling, cards, shuffle-board, speakers and other forms of entertainment. Mrs. Quail has served on the executive as secretary, as president, and currently as first vice-president.

Kemptville Home Support gives seniors the extra help they require to stay in their own homes. In addition to being on the executive of this provincially-funded organization for eight years, Mrs. Quail regularly provides transportation for seniors, not just to medical appointments but wherever they would like to go. "Anybody who contacts me, if they want to go visit somebody or anything, if I'm free, I take them," she explains. This same understanding of the need for house-bound people to have a change of scenery as often as possible motivates her work as a senior Volunteer in Service, another provincial program to increase the mobility of seniors.

Since 1978, through the Bayfield Manor Auxiliary, Mrs. Quail has helped the seniors in that retirement and nursing home in many ways. At one time, it was mending clothes for some of the residents who did not have families to help them; at another, she used to accompany the activity director when she took some of the residents bowling every week. Now, through the United Church Women, "we put on a birthday party once a month. The unit I belong to is responsible for May, June, July and August," she says.

Mrs. Quail is very active in the St. John's United Church Women, and served two years as president in the past. She also spent two years as convenor of the Outreach Commission, whose ongoing project is to provide the church with an elevator in order to make it more accessible to handicapped people.

Every Wednesday, Mrs. Quail takes several people who do not have their own means of transportation to a luncheon at Kemptville Home Support as part of its Wheels to Meals program. Afterwards, they usually go shopping on the way home. And she never goes alone to Klub 67 meetings: for those, as for Home Support's Friday cinema of VCR movies, popcorn and tea, she always picks up other seniors who would otherwise not be able to go.

Back Row (L to R): Bryan Brown, Don Helliker, Chris Brioux, Mervin Robinson, Mike Lamothe, Dan Polley, Mark Robinson
Middle (L - R): Tom Graham, Howard Leach, Ted Ward, Victor Desroches, Alan Forbes, Joe Tensen, Peter Tensen
Front (L - R): Joyce Madill, Brenda Ward, Ruth Aldham

Back Row (L - R): Case Overdulve, Joan Tensen, Victor Jarjour, Linda DesRoches, Gary Dicks, Mary Humphries
Front (L - R): Albert Beking, Grant Hendrick, Alf Van Dyke, John Russell, Bruce Loney

Back Row (L - R): Erna Finley, Amanda Casselden, Heather Gagnon, Patricia Philpotts, Lillian Leonard, Kathy Knott, Gail Gray

Front Row (L - R): Bruce Paterson, Brian Casselden, Brian Heath, Howard Hobbs, Greg Leonard, Steve Gray, Marty Gagnon, Roger Stark, Wayne Mann

RECREATION AND SPORTS
carrying on a township tradition

Community sports, a source of fun and social contact, have long been a tradition in Oxford-on-Rideau Township. More than fifty years ago, small communities within the township had baseball teams, and the games they played were a major source of entertainment for young and old alike. Today, volunteer organizers and coaches of a whole range of recreation and sports activities are helping to carry on this community spirit.

Oxford-on-Rideau Recreation Committee: Kathy Knott (chairperson), Nancy Curtis (council representative), Linda Desroches, Heather Gagnon, Gail Gray, Jean Hamlyn (council representative), Brian Heath, Pat Philpotts and Joan Tensen.

Volunteer coaches for T-ball and softball: at Oxford Mills, Gary Abson, Albert Beking, Gail and Steve Gray, Brian Heath, Claude Lapierre and Bruce Paterson; at Bishops Mills, Keith Cameron, Linda and Victor Desroches, Erna Finley, John Polley, Mervin Robinson, Doug and Irene Scott and Peter Tensen; at Burritts Rapids, Mike Daoust, Gary Dicks, Marty Gagnon, Howard Hobbs, Kathy and Verner Knott, Bob Parnell and Jay Terrill.

Skating-rink flooders and cleaners: at Bishops Mills, Victor Desroches, Tom Graham, John, Ben and Dan Polley, Mark Robinson and Joe Tensen; at Oxford Mills, Michael Bradfield, Ray and Joanne Briggs, Bryan Brown, Doug Hamilton, Brian Heath, Bruce Paterson, John Paterson, and Team Zamboni, a group of grade-six kids from Oxford-on-Rideau School.

Kemptville Soccer Club: Susan and Drew Young (president), Ted and Mary Humphries,

and Victor Jarjour represent Oxford-on-Rideau on the executive. Volunteer coaches from the township: Bill Anderson, Gary Dicks, John Hadrovic, Grant Hendrick, Louis Kelemen, Greg Leonard, Case Overdulve, Carl Patterson, John Russell, Wolfgang Stelzer and Alf Van Dyke.

Kemptville & District Minor Hockey League: Bob Brown, Steve Gray, Howard Leach, Keitha Ozga, Fred Robinson, Clara Thompson and Ted Ward are Oxford-on-Rideau executive members. Volunteer coaches from the township: Chris Brioux, Mark Bullied, Kerry Coleman, Al Forbes, Dan Hefkey, Don Helliker, Bill Holmes, Mike Lamothe, Wayne Mann, Doug Moir, Dale Philpotts, Fred Robinson, Roger Stark and Ken Thompson.

Kemptville Figure Skating Club: Brenda Ward (president), Ruth Aldham, Brenda Johnston, Barb Landenberg, Joyce Madill and Harold Workman

Tennis: Lillian Leonard and Diana Bowles

Gymnastics: Patricia Philpotts

Adult mixed softball: Amanda and Brian Casselden

Badminton: Michael Bradfield and Kevin Cameron

Oxford Downs Pony Club: Janet and Ron McLean, Betty and Ted Cooper, Linda Lee and Leo St. Louis, Gary and Isabel Blake and Joanne Dawn.

Extra-curricular sports at North Grenville District High School: Gary Bowlby (volleyball), Heather Burns (volleyball), Ted Cooper (basketball), and Carol Durie (track and field)

ARLINE RUTTER
leadership by example

Arline Rutter and her husband David moved to Canada from England in 1965 and became Canadian citizens in 1970. Arline considers the time she spends as a 4-H leader an investment in the future of the community and the country. In the ten years that she has been with 4-H, scores of young people from Oxford Mills, Bishops Mills, Oxford Station and Kemptville have come to her to learn leadership skills, gain self-confidence and have a lot of fun into the bargain. "I really feel that the young people need this," she says. "It can give them a little more self-confidence."

Because the 4-H motto is Hands On and the kids learn by doing, Arline's own experience has really been broadened with new skills she has had to learn so that she can give meaningful direction to the diverse projects she oversees. Quilting, bread making, trail blazing and kite construction are just some of these skills. The most significant addition to her repertoire of abilities, however, is teaching effectively to people between the ages of ten and twenty-one who have chosen 4-H over more hedonistic pursuits for their spare time. "You have to learn how to teach without being boring, to get things across in a fun way," she says. The club meets weekly over a period of six to eight weeks every spring and fall, and the children work on projects on a variety of subjects that include agricultural and environmental concerns, heritage and family trees, cooking, and crafts. "And you don't need a calf or horse to join!" she adds.

Arline belongs to the Grenville County Leaders' Association and has served on the executive as secretary, vice-president, president and now secretary again. In the fall of 1990 she was chosen as one of four representatives of all the 4-H clubs in Ontario to attend a national conference for 4-H leaders in Toronto. Her job as leader is made easier these days by the assistance of parent volunteers Eleanor Hossie, Betty Poirier, Michael Oomen, Irene Scott, Melodie Wynne and Sandy Hutchins.

For the last three years, Arline has been a co-ordinator and chairperson of Home Management Day, a day for women in the community during Kemptville College's annual Farmers' Week. She has also been a canvasser for the Heart and Stroke Foundation for several years. When her daughters, Caroline, twenty-one, and Kirsty, nineteen, were younger, Arline did volunteer work in their school and helped out as a leader for Guides and a mother helper for Brownies.

Back (L - R) Aaron, Don, Doug
Front - Marg

THE SCOTT FAMILY
working together for friends and neighbors

Marg and Aaron Scott and their sons, Doug and Don, have a reputation around Oxford-on-Rideau as good neighbours. As with most families, they all have different ways of working and relating to people, but they have all earned the respect and affection of the community they live in.

Their roots go back a long way on both sides. Aaron's great-grandfather Joseph Scott was born in Oxford-on-Rideau in 1823. His wife, Mary Ann Percival, was also born in the township. Aaron's dad, Harold, left the Scott homestead on Scott Road and bought their present farm at Actons Corners in 1925, the year before he married Pearl Pettapiece from Oxford Mills. Although Marg moved to Oxford-on-Rideau from Inkerman as a child in 1941, her family, the Guys, had actually been early settlers to Oxford-on-Rideau, arriving in the township in the early 1800s.

Don, a mechanic by trade, devotes a lot of his spare time to young people in the community. He leads a beef project with 4-H and is a moving force behind the Grenville County Junior Farmers Club. He was recently selected to represent the provincial organization on a six-month exchange to Australia and New Zealand in 1992. Don is now county secretary and assistant provincial director of the Grenville club. Having gone through both 4-H and Junior Farmers himself, he appreciates the impact these clubs can have on young people.

Doug has inherited the love of the land that inspired his ancestors to build a life in the raw, new country. Aside from his full-time job with the township, he runs the Scott's beef farm, enjoys hunting and wood cutting, and has ploughed in competition since the age of ten. A member of the Grenville County Ploughmen's Association

for four years and presently president, Doug hosted a ploughing match at the farm in September 1991. He was a director of the Merrickville Fair Board in 1989. A quiet man who shares his father's dislike of bureaucracy, Doug is often in the background of community events helping to make things run smoothly.

Marg, a teacher by profession, is vitality itself, and she manages to channel her high level of energy into the volunteer jobs she frequently takes on and always sees to completion. "I'm good at helping to organize social events," she says. She often plays the organ and piano at different area churches, and she has been a member of the Actons Corners Community Association for many years. Marg is a charter executive member of the Oxford-on-Rideau Historical Society, and her hard work and unsquelchable enthusiasm throughout 1991 helped spread the bicentennial spirit around the township. Her triumph for the year was the outdoor heritage displays she brought together for Founders Days in August.

Aaron is now using his retirement from thirty-five years with the Ministry of Transportation of Ontario to putter around with his collections of antique toys and machinery. A member of the Golden Triangle Steam and Antique Preservers Association, Aaron enjoys demonstrating some of his prized pieces at local fairs. "We usually take something to the Merrickville Fair and to any other community activities," says Aaron. His 1927 Waterloo threshing mill has been a star performer on many occasions, including the 1983 International Ploughing Match at Richmond, Ontario, and an old-style threshing bee in 1989 at the home of Bruce and Liz Robinson.

ERIC SMITH
always a ready smile and a pleasant manner

Crossing paths with Eric Smith is sure to make anyone's day pleasanter. Among the joys of his retirement are meeting new people, visiting with old friends and discussing just about any topic. Part of his charm is his ability to listen as well as talk.

Given the right company, Eric brims with stories about his fighter-pilot days which were launched during World War II in a versatile twin-engine bomber called a Mosquito. So exceptional was his military record and so clear are his memories of the wars and times that provided the backdrop to his military career that he has been included in a number of books such as *Sixty Years: The History of the RCAF*, *The Canadian Sabre* and *The RCAF Squadron Histories and Aircraft*.

Despite all this, Eric is no glorifier of war. "You win the war and you lose the peace," he says. "It's all so futile." He ought to know. During his twenty-seven years in the Air Force, he was awarded ten medals for his actions as a pilot in World War II and the Korean War. One of these was the Distinguished Flying Cross in 1945. Eric and Andy Mackenzie, another township resident with a colourful military background, are two of only seven pilots living in Canada who have had combat experience in two wars.

A native son of rural Navan, Ontario, Eric settled on a farm in the south-east corner of Oxford-on-Rideau in 1966, just as he was retiring from the Air Force. Piloting was not his first career, however. He obtained his First Class Teacher's Certificate from the Ottawa Normal School in 1940, and subsequently spent a year teaching grades one to eight in a one-room school at Carlsbad Springs. On July 1, 1941, with the ink barely dry on his pupils' report cards, he joined the Air Force as a pilot. At the age of twenty, he was more interested in making history than in teaching it. "I was perhaps a tad short," he recalls, "but they took me!"

Settling in Oxford-on-Rideau with wife Dinah and daughter Erin marked the end of Eric's active military career, although he still belongs to several veteran pilots' associations. He spent the next twenty years in real estate, meeting people and immersing himself in the life of the township as he went. He joined the Lions Club as well as the Kemptville Masonic Order and Royal Archmasons. He has also been a member of the Spencerville Legion and Shriners' Tunis Temple in Ottawa. During his long affiliation with St. James Anglican Church in Kemptville, he acted for five years as church warden. He has served on the Grenville County Pork Producers' Association as secretary, on the Soil and Crop Improvement Association, and as director with the Spencerville Agricultural Society.

EVAH SMITH
dignity in life, pride in heritage

Evah Smith still lives on the same South River Road farm where she was born in 1895. She belongs to the Percival family which at one time owned twelve prosperous farms between Burritts Rapids and the Catchall. Now she and her son Ivan are the only Percivals still living on the original homestead. The house, built by her father in 1893, replaced a log home that had been in the same location since the Percivals first acquired the farm.

The original owner of the fifty-acre Smith farm was a Captain Fraser of the British army. In the early 1800s, William Andrew Percival, Mrs. Smith's great-grandfather, came out from Wexford County, Ireland, and bought the land from Fraser. He established the farm which passed to his son, Andrew, Mrs. Smith's grandfather. Andrew married Martha Norton, who came from the Swann area outside Oxford Mills. Thomas, William, Norton and Maria were their children.

Thomas, Mrs. Smith's father, married Maria McDonald in 1879. Maria was one of eight children of Eliza Hogaboon and Vincent Booth McDonald, Scottish immigrants who had settled at Mallorytown. Thomas and Maria had four daughters; Evah, the baby of the family, is the only one still living. Harriet, born in 1881, married Herbert Goth and moved to Pierces Corners where they raised twelve children. The twins, Eliza and Martha, came along in 1891. Eliza never married; Martha and her husband, Alec Davidson of Brockville, had no children. All four sisters went to school in Burritts Rapids.

In 1922, Evah Percival married Andrew Smith, who had come to Canada from Scotland as a home child in 1905 at the age of fourteen. Until he joined the army during World War I, he worked on a farm west of Burritts Rapids on the north side of the river. Overseas, Andrew was captured after the Battle of Ypres and spent the duration of the war in a German prisoner-of-war camp. After he was released in 1918, he worked at the same farm until he and Evah were married. Then he moved to the Percival farm and took over its operation. It started out as a beef farm, then went to dairy around 1947. Andrew Smith died in 1956 and Ivan, their only child, has continued farming it since then. Ivan is now going back to beef from dairy.

Mrs. Smith attended the Burritts Rapids Methodist Church, which became United after church union in 1925. She was made a life member of the the United Church Women there for her years of dedicated service. "They used to call it the Ladies Aid when I was young," she says. "I held all the different offices when I was there."

She and Ivan have lived longer on the South River Road longer than any other residents from Becketts Landing to Burritts Rapids. "We've seen everyone else move in," she says.

LINDA LEE ST. LOUIS
energy and enthusiasm for rural living

"I can't imagine living anywhere else," says Linda Lee St. Louis of the 150-year-old homestead she and her husband Leo bought at Actons Corners in 1985. They were looking for a place to bring up their three young daughters — Adrienne, Olivia and Emily — in a friendly rural community with traditional values.

Linda Lee and Leo's stong interest in heritage, in the ways of the people who opened up this country, is reflected in the independent lifestyle they have developed. "Our ancestors relied largely on their own efforts to sustain themselves," she explains. "People today have lost that ability to a large extent." They have the satisfaction of knowing they can provide many of the necessities of life for themselves. Both she and Leo believe strongly in the family-run farm as a vital social and economic unit.

Linda Lee grew up on a dairy farm at Kars, Ontario, in a community that was warm and caring, and she wants her own daughters to experience that as well. "I had a happy childhood, and I want to pass that on to my children," she says. She also wants them to learn life skills like sewing, preserving and livestock tending that modern life is trying to make obsolete. Leo combines carpentry and masonry with other traditional skills in the ongoing maintenance of their farm.

Linda Lee's parents, Hugh Lindsay and Coral Scharf, both come from long-established families in Rideau Township. "I grew up in an atmosphere where I was aware of my roots," she says. The tales she was told as a child about her ancestors made them seem real and alive to her. "An enthusiasm for heritage doesn't come from dry facts," she points out.

In February 1991, during Heritage Week, Linda Lee co-ordinated an exhibit on the various aspects of life of the settlers who lived in Oxford-on-Rideau from 1791 to 1841. Over a two-day period, hundreds of children from the township's two elementary schools visited the written, pictorial and hands-on displays which Linda Lee, dressed in period costume, helped bring to life for them. She attributes the tremendous positive response, at least in part, to her eye-catching finery, complete with parasol, hoop skirt and plumed hat.

"Costumes really make an impact on people," she says. She designs and sews her own dresses to be authentic to a particular time. Linda Lee spent a lot of time during the bicentennial year helping dozens of people get outfitted with costumes for Founders Days and other heritage events held about the township.

Since coming to Actons Corners, the St. Louis family has been active in the Oxford Downs Pony Club and in St. Andrew's Presbyterian Church in Oxford Mills where Linda Lee is superintendant and a teacher of Sunday school. She is a director and charter member of the Oxford-on-Rideau Historical Society and serves on the social committee of the Actons Corners Community Association. "You do it because you want to, because you enjoy it," she says.

AB STOREY

committed to the tradition of the family farm

Ab Storey is the fourth generation of his family to farm on the same land on the far east side of Oxford-on-Rideau Township. Although the Scottish name has been spelled Story, Storie and Storrie in the past, it has been stabilized as Storey for many years now, says Ab.

His great-grandfather, Robert Storey, came to Oxford-on-Rideau Township from Eccles, Scotland, over a hundred and sixty years ago. On March 3, 1829, at the age of thirty, Robert bought about fifty acres of land from one William Bartholomew for the sum of thirty-two pounds, ten shillings. Ab still has the original deed. Robert purchased additional land from Bartholomew in 1854, bringing the farm up to about a hundred acres. Today, it has shrunk to ninety-four acres as some of the land was expropriated in the past for a railroad and a highway.

Robert and his wife Margaret built a log house on the south-east corner of the property. Ab believes the existing stone house was built during the 1830s when the Rideau Canal was being constructed. Certainly it was in existence by the time the farm was passed on to Ab's grandfather, Benjamin, born in 1844, the youngest of seven children. Benjamin married Charlotte Froats, and had three children, Byron (1898), Carrie (1901) and Robert (1904). The farm passed to Byron in his turn. He married Ethel Mather and had two children, Robert Albert (Ab) and Elizabeth, who now lives at Odessa.

When Ab started school around 1930, the Mill's School had just been rebuilt after a fire. The previous spring, Byron had got his first tractor. Ab remembers that day clearly although he was only about six at the time. "Father got the tractor from North Gower. It was Arbour Day and it was the day the Mill's School burned." The tractor was one of the first Fordsons, a model-T type with steel wheels and a coil for each cylinder.

Ab walked or biked the three miles to Kemptville High School during the war. The policy then was to let the children of farmers out of school early so that they could help with spring planting, and Ab never had to write any exams. After finishing high school, Ab occasionally held jobs such as truck driving off the farm, but farming with Byron was always his main occupation. He has been farming alone since Byron died in 1983, and now specializes in beef. "I never liked milking," he confesses.

The stores in Kemptville would be open Saturday night when Ab was younger, and families from the outlying areas would come in to do their shopping and socialize. There used to be a dance pavilion south on Prescott Street. People would gather at the ice-cream booth at the corner of Prescott and Clothier, and sometimes a travelling salesman would play his guitar and show off his pet black bear to entice people to buy his wares.

"When I was younger, everybody worked together," Ab says. "If you needed help for a day, you helped your neighbour and he helped you." Nobody had much money then but it didn't matter much because neighbours were always willing to help.

Ransford Streight is shown with Brooke Meikle

RANSFORD STREIGHT
safe passage for our school children

Ransford Streight has been driving kids from Bishops Mills to Oxford Mills since Oxford-on-Rideau School opened in 1964. "I'm the only one still driving (a school bus) of the seven that started at that time," he muses. Esther Weir once wrote in the Kemptville *Advance* that Ransford reminded her of the Pied Piper, collecting all the children in Bishops and taking them away every morning. The difference, of course, was that he always brought them home safely to their families after school. "I've carried several lads off the bus fast asleep," he says of the bus routes that sometimes, in his opinion, had kindergarten children on the bus far too long. "The first few years were the best bus-driving years," says Ransford, who finds that children had better bus manners twenty-five years ago than they do now.

Ransford had driven just about every kind of vehicle except a school bus when he first tendered for a route. To get his licence in Kemptville, he borrowed a school bus from a friend in Throoptown and passed the driving test with ease. Once he had the licence and the job, he got himself a brand new school bus for seven thousand dollars. Today, he points out, essentially the same bus would cost ten times that amount new. "I bought it at Stirling and drove it home," he recalls.

Although Ransford puts a lot of time and energy into school-bus driving, it is in fact a sideline for him. He is a partner in Streight Farms, a Bishops Mills dairy operation, along with his wife Marion, his son Robert and wife Liz, and his brother Ralph and wife Marjorie. Ransford's other son, David, helps out while attending Kemptville College and plans to be a partner when he graduates. They milk close to sixty Holsteins now, growing all their feed on about four hundred acres, eighty of them rented from a neighbour.

The first Streight came from Ireland and settled in neighbouring Augusta Township in 1866. He established a homestead which is still in the family. In 1937, John Streight, his wife Florence Davies and their six sons moved to the present Streight farm near Bishops Mills. They still use the Augusta farm, about three miles away, making Ransford and Ralph the fourth and Robert and David the fifth generations of Streights to farm the original homestead there.

Ransford married Marion Van Camp from Garretton in 1952. Their three children, Robert, Nancy (Tousaw) and David, all live at Bishops Mills.

PAT STROULGER
carrying on a family tradition

Pat Stroulger's name has become almost synonymous with the Burritts Rapids community hall. Particularly in the last nine years, Pat has been a moving force behind the upgrading of the hall and many of the community activities based there.

Since settling in Burritts Rapids as a child, Pat has always thrown herself into village activities, as did her parents and two sisters, Andrea and Lynda. Her father, Cameron, bought Kidd's store in 1962, eventually operating it from their home until his death in 1974. In his day, Cam was postmaster, local paper columnist, United Church elder, director of the community-hall board and member of the Merrickville Masonic Lodge. May, Pat's mother, one of a group of extremely active women in Burritts Rapids, was also an elder in the church and belonged to groups such as the United Church Women, Women's Institute, hall board and so on. "Whenever anything needed to be done, the ladies did it," remembers Pat. Later, May assisted Pat in her community work, and she has been greatly missed about the area since she died in April, 1989.

Pat's executive ability shone when she took on the roles of instigator, fund raiser and general foreman of the new addition to the community hall. Pat realized that the hall would better serve the community if it were expanded and had a better kitchen, as many of the activities held there involved the preparation of meals on a large scale. As luck would have it, she heard through the grapevine that the large wooden sets built for *The Boy in Blue*, a movie that was partially shot near the locks in the village, were going to be removed and trashed. Pat acted quickly and worked out a contract with the film company for the village to remove and keep the sets.

While the lumber mellowed for a couple of years in Debbie Gerrard's garage, Pat set about fund raising to match a provincial grant. She sought donations from both Rideau and Oxford-on-Rideau, the two townships Burritts Rapids occupies, as well as from all members of the Burritt family, who have moved far afield since their venerable ancestor arrived some two hundred years ago. "We scrounged as much as we could, and we badgered the building companies into giving us discounts and holding our notes endlessly," she recalls. Once the funding was in place, the hall took two years to build, during which time Pat coordinated the largely volunteer force that worked on it. "I'd never tackle anything that size again!" she vows. "It was a lot of work but we were very pleased when we were finished."

Pat has also served on the hall board for several years, as a secretary in the past and now in her third term as president. This past June, she and neighbour Don MacCraken hosted their second golf tournament as a hall fund raiser on a nine-hole course they made on their adjoining properties. She is also on the Board of Directors of the Merrickville Medical Centre. Not surprisingly, Pat was honoured in 1988 with a Volunteer Service Award from the Provincial Government and a Certificate of Merit from the Government of Canada, both for her efforts on behalf of the Burritts Rapids community.

The real work on the hall was done by many members of the community, says Pat, who sees herself more as a catalyst than an activist. "When the village works together, you can accomplish lots."

HILLAIS SUDDABY
for the love of the land

Looking back at nearly fifty years of dairy farming at Oxford Mills, Hillais Suddaby credits hard work and sensible decisions for his success as a breeder and showman of pure-bred Holsteins. Now a widower living in Kemptville, he has time to reflect on those busy, productive years. "There's a tremendous amount of satisfaction to be gained from doing work you enjoy," he says. "I'd do it all again."

Hillais grew up on a farm in Mountain Township just east of Heckston. In 1938, he married Myrtle Tompkins from Millars Corners. For three years, the couple rented the stone house now owned by Abercrombies on the north side of Oxford Mills. They shared the farming operation there with the owner, Mistress Elsie Dean, in a fifty/fifty partnership.

In 1941, the Suddabys bought Ed Littlejohn's farm, just down the road from where they were renting. The six two-year-old heifers they brought with them were the start of their award-winning Myrhill herd.

Except for the last few years before they sold the farm, Hillais and Myrtle did the farm work themselves with the help of a schoolboy at haying time. Their daughter, Gail, often pitched in as well. They usually milked between twenty-eight and thirty cows and grew all the hay, oats and barley needed to feed their animals. "My theory was that the cows had to milk on what we could produce off the farm," Hillais says.

The Myrhill herd was built up with an eye to both milk production and conformation of the breed. Choosing which heifers to keep and which to cull was all-important to Hillais' breeding program. "You can't breed top cattle if you're selling all the best heifers off," he points out.

Hillais showed the Myrhill cattle regularly at the Grenville County Holstein Show and the Ottawa Winter Fair, and occasionally at the Central Canada Exhibition. For twelve years in succession at the Grenville County Black and White Show, Hillais was both premier breeder and premier exhibitor. In other years, he was often one or the other. In 1968, he was awarded the Master Breeder Shield by the Canadian Holstein Association.

Hillais served as the Grenville County representative on the board of directors of Eastern Breeders for twenty-two years. He still attends meetings of the Eastern Ontario Soil and Crop Improvement Association which presented him with the H. Harris McNish Memorial Award in 1964 "in recognition of outstanding leadership in agriculture." He is also a member of the County Federation of Agriculture and the Kemptville Orange Lodge.

Hillais and Myrtle sold the farm in 1986. "The hired man quit. We were both over seventy and felt it was too late to break in another one," he jokes. Until her death two years later, Myrtle was an active member of the Oxford Mills Women's Institute. Hillais still attends Oxford Mills United Church occasionally. He was a member of session there for many years and Myrtle used to be organist and an active member of the United Church Women.

Dorothea Brown, Marian Tallman and Muriel Hill

MARIAN TALLMAN, DOROTHEA BROWN AND MURIEL HILL
always at the heart of Burritts Rapids

Burritts Rapids has been the richer for the efforts of the Hyland sisters. Marian Tallman, Dorothea Brown and Muriel Hill have all retired from taking an active role in village life, but for many people they are still part of the heart of that community. For years, whatever was happening — parties, suppers, weddings, funerals, picnics — these three, like so many others in the village, were always ready to lend a hand.

Their parents, Joseph Hyland, a carpenter by trade, and Evelyn Whiting, moved to Burritts Rapids from neighbouring Marlborough township in 1910 when they were married. The Hylands, originally from Ireland, had been early settlers around Pierces Corners. Joseph and Evelyn had three sons as well: Keith, like his sisters, still lives in Burritts Rapids; George and Clarence, also long-time village residents, have passed away. All the Hyland children went to the two-storey Burritts Rapids school. Marian has always lived in her parents' first home, which was built by the Burritts.

In 1939, Marian married Guy Tallman. As teenagers, she and Muriel had worked at the woollen mill in Burritts Rapids, and during World War II, Marian was able to have a machine from the mill set up in her home where she could sew the toes in socks and care for her young brood at the same time. Not long after the birth of their fifth child, Guy died at the age of thirty-two. As soon as all the children were in school, Marian worked at the Rideau Regional Centre in Smiths Falls.

"Children weren't so demanding as they are today," she smiles. She now boasts eleven grandchildren and one great-grandson.

The community hall has long been the centre of Burritts Rapids' social and recreational activities. "You've no idea the crowds we used to have at the dances there," recalls Marian, who has been active on the hall committee for most of her life. She also has strong ties with the Women's Institute. "I've belonged to that since I was about eighteen," she says. She held every office and stayed with the Burritts Rapids branch until it disbanded recently. Marian also spent about five years on the parish council of Christ Church, retiring in 1990.

Dorothea, like Marian, served for years with the Women's Institute and like their mother, was an active member of the Ladies Orange Benevolent Association. She taught school from the age of eighteen, spending much of her thirty-five-year career at her old school in Burritts Rapids, and later at the new school in Oxford Mills. In 1940, she married Stewart Brown; the couple has always lived in Burritts Rapids. To date, their two children have produced six grandchildren and they, in turn, three great-grandchildren.

Muriel married Lloyd Hill in 1956. Despite the time involved in commuting to her government job in Ottawa, Muriel always found time to help out with any community activities that were going on. She and Lloyd have one son and three grandchildren.

Margaret and Mel Thomas

MEL THOMAS
preserving life's past for tomorrow

Mel Thomas's 1945, three-ton Chevy Maple Leaf, which he has named Old Rampike, is getting to be a familiar sight at area fairs. Mel has restored the old truck to almost mint condition and uses it to transport and display his remarkable collection of tools, equipment and artifacts from the logging industry. "What we have would date from about 1890," he says. With the assistance of his wife, Margaret, Mel has taken his display as far as Arnprior and Perth. He never charges: being able to share with others his fascinating collection and memories of the years he spent logging is payment enough.

He has every conceivable tool, from axes to winches, that was used to convert standing timber into usable lumber, and just about any object, from tin cup to dinner gong, that was part of life in the logging camps of yesteryear. His own interest in logging began at the age of sixteen when he spent the first of several winters at logging camps in Northern Ontario. When he married Margaret Dickson in 1942, they were busy with the mixed farm they bought at their native Antrim. However, in 1945, to meet the demand for lumber to build wartime housing all over the province, Mel started up his own logging business which he operated winters in the Pakenham mountains. "Lumber was scarce," he recalls. "They were just hounding us for it all the time." By 1953, he got out of the logging business when his supply of available timber and the demand for lumber was low.

During his logging and farming days, Mel started a third line of work which was eventually to bring him to the Kemptville area. In 1949, he became an inseminating technician in his own neighbourhood for the newly started Eastern Breeders. By 1964, he had become Director of Promotion and Information. "I travelled throughout the world to get markets for Eastern Breeders semen," he explains. He visited most European countries, many in South America, India and many more, helping indigenous people to breed superior cattle that gave more milk on less feed. Shortly after his appointment, he, Margaret and their four children moved to Kemptville. In 1972, they moved to Becketts Landing.

In 1981, two years after his retirement, Mel wrote Canada's first published history of artificial insemination in cattle. The book, entitled *Artificial Insemination, Eastern Ontario 1935 to 1981* tells about the beginnings of Eastern Breeders. "Artificial insemination was first developed in Canada," explains Mel. "This is one area where Canada was a world leader."

Mel is a thirty-one-year veteran with the Rotary Club, and aside from being on and chairing many committees over the years, he was president of the Kemptville club in 1978. "A lot of my time with Rotary I did work in other countries," he says. When he was travelling for Eastern Breeders, the two commitments dovetailed nicely. Other Rotary clubs, including Cornwall, Port Hope and Kitchener, approached Mel to set up programs for them to help other countries. "Most of it had to do with the cattle industry," says Mel, who has now retired from his active position with the club.

LOUISE THOMPSON
actively and creatively promoting goodwill

Louise Thompson finds that her family, her home and a full-time business to oversee are more than enough to keep her hopping. Yet giving some of her time and talents to the community is very important to her, and she will always find the time to help others.

Louise's Goodwill Christmas Tree has given the spirit of giving a real boost around the Kemptville area. When she set up her first tree in a Kemptville store in 1986, her thought was to provide toys and clothing for some of the needy children in the area. She is delighted at the project's success. "I never dreamed it would take off like that!" she smiles. Now the Goodwill Christmas Tree provides "a little bit of extra cheer" to anyone in the community who is alone at Christmas as well as to needy families, and it has become so big that Louise has asked the Kemptville Kinnette Club to take it over.

"I fashioned the idea from the Angel Tree in Ottawa," Louise explains. In the fall, she obtains the names of potential gift recipients from sources such as nursing homes, chronic-care facilities and welfare agencies. Then the real work begins. The tree, set up in a variety store in Kemptville, is decorated with sealed envelopes coded with numbers for anonymity. In each envelope are details about the age, size and tastes of one of these gift recipients. Members of the public pick an envelope, buy and wrap suitable gifts, and return them, with the code number, to the tree. Louise sees that the gifts are delivered in time for Christmas.

"It's not meant to be for the needy only," she stresses. "It's also for people who are alone, at home or in nursing homes."

Community response has been almost overwhelming. Many groups, instead of swapping gifts among themselves, now pool their money and buy gifts for the Goodwill Tree. "The schools have gotten into it wholeheartedly each year in the class-rooms," says Louise. For groups of children, including Guides and Scouts, she likes to match up the age of the recipient with that of the donors.

Louise has also been heavily involved with the Cancer Society for six years now. She started off co-chairing the annual April campaign, and then became chairperson of the Kemptville chapter for two years. She has helped out with a lot of fund-raising activities, including the annual Fred Scambati Golf Tournament which netted over $12,000 for cancer research in 1991.

Fashion shows are a popular fund-raising activity for many local charitable organizations, and Louise has often shared her special expertise with floral arrangements to help make these affairs successful.

Working with teenage girls as a Pathfinder leader is something Louise really enjoys. "I have a ball with the girls!" she says. She sees her role as that of a "lifter," supplementing the more serious activities led by the hard-working Guiders with doses of enthusiasm and fun. For years, Louise helped out at guide camp for local Girl Guide packs.

(L - R): Garnet, Lois, Harold

THE TOMPKINS FAMILY
seven generations on the family farm

Seven generations of Tompkins living on the same farm is probably what Denis Tompkins had in mind when he and his young family arrived from Ireland in 1817. Garnet Tompkins still has his great-great- grandfather's Crown deed to the farm, located on Tompkins Road near Millars Corners. The original hundred acres increased as additional parcels were added to it; today the Tompkins property is two hundred acres. Mixed farming has carried on down through the years. Today, Harold, one of Garnet's two sons, raises dairy heifers. Neil, his wife Helena and their two sons, Barry and Ronnie, have their own home on the land, but they do not farm.

Garnet's wife Lois, a Norton by birth, is also from a family long-established in the area. Two Norton Roads were named after her father, George. The Nortons first settled in Oxford-on-Rideau during the 1830s.

Tradition is strong in the family. John Tompkins, grandson of Denis and grandfather of Garnet, helped lay the corner-stone for St. Anne's Church in Oxford Station and became the first warden there in 1879. John's son Benjamin was also a warden, as is Garnet now, and the three generations of Tompkins have completed more than one hundred consecutive years as warden at St. Anne's. Garnet's great-great-grandfather, Denis, was a charter member of the Edwardsburg Loyal Orange Lodge, founded in 1854. Garnet, too, has been a member for sixty-three years.

The house where Garnet, Lois and Harold live was built in 1898. Prior to that, the family lived in a log house which had been moved before Garnet's time. Garnet went to school at Millars Corners, known as SS No 17 then. Lois attended Adams School at Van Allens Corners. The two met in Heckston.

They recall slower, poorer-yet-gentler times when farmers got together to help one another with sawing, threshing and cutting corn. "The women had lots of fun baking," Lois remembers. Now almost all farmers have their own machinery, even though they use most of it for such a short time each season. "People don't mix like they used to," says Garnet.

Lois, an active member of the Anglican Church Women, used to belong to the Women's Institute when there was a branch in Oxford Station. Harold is a charter member and vice-president of the recently formed Oxford-on-Rideau Historical Society. He co-ordinated Founders Days, the two-day bicentennial celebration held in Oxford Mills in early August. People from all over the township took part in the event which included exhibits of vintage collections, a steam show, a parade, children's games and competitions, an ecumenical church service and a dinner-dance.

Note: The community lost a good citizen when Garnet Tompkins passed away on September 30, 1991.

BRUCE TURNER
working to help man and nature coexist

Bruce Turner has devoted most of his life to the proper management of wildlife. A former game warden with the Ministry of Natural Resources, Bruce is aware of the dangers of uncontrolled wild animal species, both to people and to other animal populations. Rabies outbreaks and the flooding of good land are two of the possible consequences of allowing animals to flourish unchecked. He believes that hunters are crucial in keeping the numbers of deer, foxes, rabbits, racoons, wolves and beaver in balance. "Wildlife will be healthy and well managed if it is harvested in a controlled fashion," he says.

Perhaps growing up on the Holland Marsh north of Toronto, an area singularly devoid of any major wildlife by virtue of its flat treelessness, contributed to Bruce's fascination with the tall timber of Northern Ontario. At any rate, after being discharged from the armed forces at the end of World War II, he became a game warden and spent many years based in remote places such as Kapuskasing, Hearst and Gogama. He spent long periods of time in the bush studying the habits of the wildlife there and working on devising laws that would produce healthy animals through sensible means and times for hunting. "I enjoyed those times in the woods," he says.

Since coming to Kemptville in 1963, Bruce has worked through the Ministry of Natural Resources on many special projects such as harvesting beaver and finding better methods of controlling coyotes and wolves. Since his retirement, Bruce has continued to be actively involved in advocating the proper control of wildlife through sensible hunting practices. When the future of deer hunting in the area appeared to be threatened in the mid-'80s by the actions of a few careless hunters, Bruce helped set up the Oxford-on-Rideau Hunters' Council to make sure hunters stayed off private property and respected the hunting laws. The Hunters' Council has been very successful in reducing friction between landowners and hunters. "We've all got to live together and we've all got to help each other," explains Bruce.

Shortly after moving to this area, Bruce began sharing his knowledge and experience of the wilds with the Boy Scouts and Girl Guides by organizing canoe trips in Algonquin Park along with Alf Campbell and others. He began when his own children, Susan and Don, were young, and he carried on for about ten years, so much did he enjoy the experience.

"I love canoeing," says Bruce. When a bad back made portaging almost impossible, he designed and built several very light canoes. Made from Ontario cedar covered with fibreglass, with seats of butter-nut and gunwales of elm, Bruce's own sixteen-foot canoe weighs only twenty-eight pounds.

A born story-teller, Bruce is able to refresh his memory about the details of his incredible experiences from the diary he kept during his thirty-three years as a game warden with the Ministry of Natural Resources.

MELVIN WEEDMARK
collector of memories

If people of future generations were to browse through Melvin Weedmark's personal archive collection, which was started by his mother, they would have a very accurate and detailed picture of what life has been like in Oxford-on-Rideau for the last eighty years. Some fifty scrap-books are filled with photographs, newspaper clippings, letters, cards, tickets, legal documents, permits, licences, bills, receipts, invoices and more. From newspapers, he keeps all pictures, news stories, birth notices, wedding and engagement write-ups, and obituaries that relate to the area. "Obituaries generally list who the family was. It's a real history," he says. Not much of significance has happened in the township that Melvin doesn't have thoroughly documented in his scrap-books. A member of both the Kemptville & District and Oxford-on-Rideau Historical Societies, he has also written out many of his memories of what life in the area was like when he was younger.

Melvin was born in Oxford Mills, the only child of Horatio Melvin Weedmark and Ruby Blanche Davis. Horatio left cheese making in the mid-1920s when he bought a farm at Actons Corners. As a boy, Melvin earned enough money for the family's first radio by buying roosters at a cent apiece and later selling them for a dollar each. Mrs. Nellie Main, Mrs. Hazel Latimer and (now Rev.) Wesley Hutton, the three teachers who taught Melvin at the Actons Corners School, SS No 6, are still alive, although about half his former class-mates are now deceased.

One day, on his way to school as a boy, Melvin found a little swarm of bees. He moved them into a hive but they didn't make it through the winter. The following spring, Melvin's father bought him a new colony, the beginning of his fifty-three-year-long career in honey production. His honey won him many first prizes at area fairs. "The bees are the only thing I miss at the farm," admits Melvin, who sold the farmhouse along with part of the acreage in 1985. At the peak of his honey production, he had seventy-five colonies. He recalls a time when no one wanted buckwheat honey, and to get rid of it, he sold it at a hundred pounds for $5.00 instead of the ten cents a pound fetched by white honey.

Since moving to Kemptville after he sold the farmhouse, Melvin has become the sponsor of Uncle Mel's, a team in the Kemptville Ladies Fastball League. "I always liked ball games," he says. Before World War II, when he was a teenager, Melvin and his friends from Actons Corners had a mixed ball team that played against another team from the River Road every Tuesday and Friday evening.

Melvin now attends the United Church in Oxford Mills where he was enrolled as a Sunday School student at the age of one. He keeps the certificate in one of his scrap-books. However, from the mid-1920s to 1963, he went to the small United Church that used to be at Actons Corners. Melvin was on the Board of Trustees of the Actons Corners Church when it was sold and removed to Bishops Mills to become part of the Pentecostal Church there.

In 1988, Melvin became a volunteer with Home Support, providing transportation to seniors for medical appointments. He also visits many people he knows in Bayfield Manor. "I try to go up once a week," he says.

(L - R): Heather, Jennifer, Chad, Harold

HEATHER WESTENDORP
getting back to basics

Heather Westendorp and her husband Harold are setting an example which offers hope to people caught in the trap of trying to live beyond their means. The Westendorps' life-style echoes their philosophy that any family can have the best things in life - being happy, healthy and together - without drowning in debt. They have been thereand back, and now they are sharing the experience with others.

In 1990,Heather wrote and published *How to Live on $16,000 aYear*, based on their own experiences changing from a high-rolling couple with a crushing $22,000 debt to a home-owning family of four with a simple life-style and a manageable debt load. The bookgives advice to people of all ages on everything from finances to environmental issues, focusing on learning to live within a realistic budget.

Alongwith the national media attention the book has attracted have come invitations and requests for Heather, and sometimes her family as well, to make public appearances and give lectures. These she normally does, asking only travelling expenses in return. She is presently involved with the Futures Pre-Employment Preparation Program, and has also been speaking about her book at five Futures satellites in the area.

Heather urges young people to be self-sufficient and to choose work over welfare. "If someone is on welfare, they're not encouraged to work because minimum wage is less than welfare," Heather points out. "I think there has to be a balance created economically for people to get out and become self-sufficient earners." So strongly does she feel about this that she wrote a second book, *Canada: Who Cares??*, that came out in September, 1991.

Meeting people during her talks and lectures after her first book, Heather realized that many people actually fear the government. She decided to demystify the system by explaining step by step how it works. "I want people to feel a little bit more comfortable dealing with the government, and I want the government to be better organized when it comes to dealing with people," she explains.

In addition to her family responsibilities, writing and lecturing, Heather presently sits on the provincial Children's Advisory Committee and has also joined the Kemptville Kinnettes where she is treasurer.

"I like doing community things," says Heather. "I feel that's important."

MERLIN WILSON
an appreciation of the simple beauty of the past

The quality, variety and sheer numbers of Merlin Wilson's oil paintings — including floral designs, portraits and what he calls "rustic rurals" — suggest a long lifetime of artistic training. In fact, Merlin did his first painting just over twenty years ago.

"It all started in the kitchen," he recalls. His wife Jean was finishing up a painting and Merlin, intrigued by the colours, decided to try a painting of his own. "I did an autumn scene," he says. "It was awful, but I thought it was fun!" With Jean's help, he developed his talent. "It's been trial and error," he says. He has long enjoyed sharing his work with others, and many of his paintings are displayed in public buildings and private homes across Canada as well as in the United States and other countries. He has organized, with other artists, two well-attended public art shows at his home. He has also donated paintings to many organizations, including the Heart and Stroke Foundation and the Kemptville District Hospital.

Merlin's interest in old farm buildings as subjects for his paintings comes from an appreciation of his heritage. All his paternal great-grandparents lived near Merrickville. In the 1890s, his paternal grandparents built the house and developed the farm just west of Merrickville where Merlin was born and raised. The farm is now operated by Merlin's younger brother Trevor and his family.

Another hobby of Merlin's is collecting and restoring old horse-drawn vehicles. He has made the day for many brides and grooms by taxiing them in his fringed surrey or Irish governess-cart hitched to one of his ponies.

After graduating from veterinary medicine at Guelph in 1955, Merlin married Jean Dougall, a class-mate of his from grade one through high school. Merlin was associated with the Belleville Animal Hospital until the fall of 1957, when he joined the staff of the Eastern Ontario Cattle Breeding Association, now Eastern Breeders Inc., as a field supervisor and veterinary consultant. This was before the days of frozen semen, and he covered a large territory talking to breeders and trying to help them improve conception rates among their stock. "I guess you could call me a bovine gynaecologist!" he laughs. By 1967, Merlin had become assistant manager of E.B.I., and from 1982 until his retirement in 1986, he was general manager. He is a past president of the Ontario association of Animal Breeders and served for a number of years on the executive of the Canadian Association of Animal Breeders.

When his daughters, Catharine and Julie, were children, Merlin helped set up the Oxford Downs Pony Club. He came up with the club name and designed its logo. Always a strong supporter of St. John's United Church, Merlin recently retired after thirty years on the board. During his years of service, he chaired many committees. And in his years with the Kemptville Lions Club, he has been secretary and president.

Oxford-on-Rideau Township

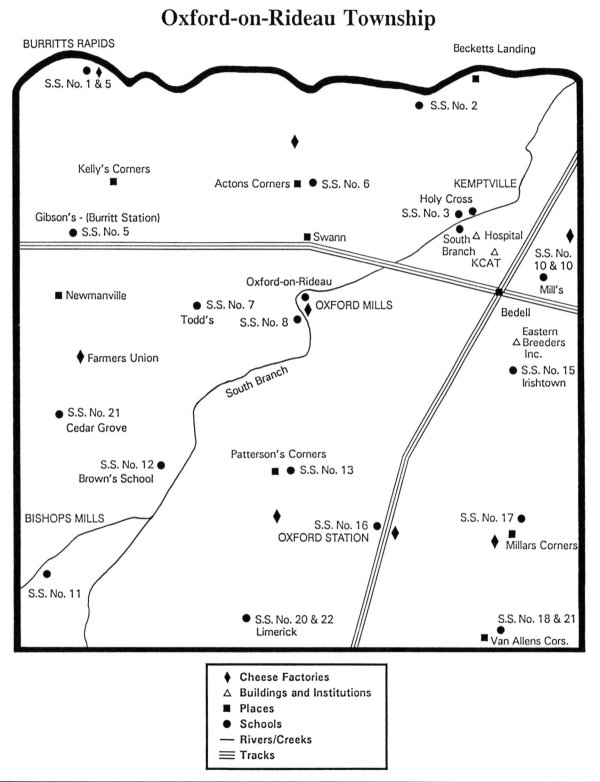

BURRITTS RAPIDS

S.S. No. 1 & 5

Becketts Landing

S.S. No. 2

Kelly's Corners

Actons Corners • S.S. No. 6

KEMPTVILLE

Holy Cross
S.S. No. 3

Gibson's - (Burritt Station)
• S.S. No. 5

South △ Hospital
Branch △
KCAT

S.S. No.
10 & 10

Mill's

■ Swann

Oxford-on-Rideau

■ Newmanville

S.S. No. 7
Todd's

OXFORD MILLS

S.S. No. 8

Bedell

Eastern
△ Breeders
Inc.

• S.S. No. 15
Irishtown

♦ Farmers Union

South Branch

• S.S. No. 21
Cedar Grove

S.S. No. 12 •
Brown's School

Patterson's Corners
■ • S.S. No. 13

BISHOPS MILLS

S.S. No. 16
OXFORD STATION

S.S. No. 17 •

Millars Corners

• S.S. No. 11

• S.S. No. 20 & 22
Limerick

S.S. No. 18 & 21
■ Van Allens Cors.

♦ Cheese Factories
△ Buildings and Institutions
■ Places
● Schools
— Rivers/Creeks
≡ Tracks

Index

About the Author

Elizabeth Irving is a freelance writer who has written mainly about local people and events. A resident of Oxford-on-Rideau Township for eleven years, she has met a wide variety of people across the township through her writing endeavors and her participation in community groups and organizations. *In Good Company* i s Elizabeth's first book, born of her appreciation of the many good people in the township where both her children have always lived.

About the Photographer

Betty Cooper has lived and taught school in Oxford-on-Rideau township for twenty years. Her favourite art form, photography, makes an excellent blend of her love of people and love of expression. Because of her strong respect for the people and the traditional values of Oxford-on-Rideau Township, the photography in this book was a labour of love.